*Articles of
Faith,
Articles of
Peace*

About Brookings

The Brookings Institution is a private nonprofit organization devoted to research, education, and publication on important issues of domestic and foreign policy. Its principal purpose is to bring knowledge to bear on the current and emerging policy problems facing the American people.

A board of trustees is responsible for general supervision of the Institution and safeguarding of its independence. The president is the chief administrative officer and bears final responsibility for the decision to publish a manuscript as a Brookings book. In reaching this judgment, the president is advised by the director of the appropriate Brookings research program and a panel of expert readers who report in confidence on the quality of the work. Publication of a work signifies that it is deemed a competent treatment worthy of public consideration but does not imply endorsement of conclusions or recommendations. The Institution itself does not take positions on policy issues.

Articles of Faith, Articles of Peace

The Religious Liberty Clauses
and the
American Public Philosophy

James Davison Hunter
Os Guinness
editors

The Brookings Institution
Washington, D.C.

Copyright © 1990 by
THE BROOKINGS INSTITUTION
1775 Massachusetts Avenue, N.W., Washington, D.C. 20036

Library of Congress Cataloging-in-Publication data

Articles of faith, articles of peace : the religious liberty clauses
and the American public philosophy / James Davison Hunter
and Os Guinness, editors.

   p.   cm.

  ISBN 0-8157-3828-5 (alk. paper)

   1. Freedom of religion—United States. 2. Church and
state—United States. 3. Religious tolerance—United States.
I. Hunter, James Davison. II. Guinness, Os.

KF4783.A97 1990

342.73'0852—dc20

[347.302852]   90-32509

                                             CIP

9 8 7 6 5 4 3 2 1

The paper used in this publication meets the minimum re-
quirements of the American National Standard for Information
Sciences—Permanence of Paper for Printed Library Materials,
ANSI Z39.48-1984.

Set in Linotron Caslon No. 2
Composition by Graphic Composition, Inc.
Athens, Georgia
Printing R. R. Donnelley and Sons Co.
Harrisonburg, Virginia
Book design by Ken Sabol

Foreword

IF THERE WAS A recurring criticism of the Bicentennial of the Declaration of Independence in 1976, it was that too often it represented celebration without education. The result, one observer wrote with sorrow, was that Americans were left with little more than "tons of red-white-and-blue junk, that made advertisers and commercial hucksters rich, but neither enriched the spirit nor nourished the understanding of the American people."

Under the tireless leadership of former Chief Justice Warren E. Burger, it was determined from the beginning that this would not be the case with the Bicentennial of the United States Constitution. Celebration needed to be matched not only by education but by reaffirmation. Minds as well as hearts had to be engaged. In the case of the vexed but vital religious liberty clauses of the First Amendment, an element of national reconciliation was needed as well as celebration and reaffirmation. To this end, some of the nation's best minds were engaged to rethink the issues concerning religious liberty and American public life.

The plans for this book were laid in the fall of 1987 as one of the cornerstone projects of the celebration and reaffirmation of the religious liberty clauses of the First Amendment. The Brookings Institution joined the Center on Religion and Society, the University of Virginia, and the Virginia Commission on the Bicentennial of the U.S. Constitution as a cohost of a national symposium organized by the Williamsburg Charter Foundation and held in April 1988 at the University of Virginia. This book is derived from that symposium, a gathering made up of a wide spectrum of scholars, religious leaders, and church-state experts and activists.

The editors would like to acknowledge their profound gratitude to the following people, organizations, and foundations that provided invaluable support for this project, both in its published form and at the symposium. A. James Reichley of Brookings, along with Richard John Neuhaus, John Seel, and the editors organized the structure of the symposium and volume. The Alonzo L. McDonald Family Fund and AVENIR®, Inc., along with the J. M. Foundation, the Esther A. and Joseph Klingenstein Fund, the Metropolitan Life Foundation, the Templeton Foundation, and Wheat First Securities, offered the generous financial support that made the project possible. The editors would also like to thank Amy C. Boucher for her administrative assistance. At Brookings, Theresa B. Walker edited the manuscript, Kieron Swaine verified it, and Florence Robinson prepared the index.

The concerns of this book would have been well appreciated by Robert Brookings, the St. Louis businessman who founded the Brookings Institution. Although the Institution has become known mainly for its application of the social sciences to issues of public policy, the broader social concerns of the founder have also been honored over the years. This book on religious liberty and American public life is thus very much at home in the broader tradition of Brookings scholarship. More important, it addresses issues and challenges that are critical to the nation's future and well-being.

Of course, the views expressed in this book are those of the authors and should not be ascribed to the persons and organizations whose assistance is acknowledged above or to the trustees, officers, or staff members of the Brookings Institution.

BRUCE K. MACLAURY
President
The Brookings Institution

Contents

 ONE

Introduction

OS GUINNESS

GEORGE WASHINGTON'S HOME, Mount Vernon, is among the nation's most visited sites. But one of the most fascinating things at Mount Vernon is one of the least noticed—the key to the Bastille, the forbidding Paris fortress whose fall on July 14, 1789, became the symbol of the French Revolution.

The key hangs in the hall at Mount Vernon, oversized for its classically proportioned surroundings and often overlooked. But it once spoke eloquently for the highest hopes in both nations. Six weeks after the ratification of the U.S. Constitution in September 1787, Jefferson rejoiced at the meeting of the Estates General and the prospect of applying revolutionary American principles to France. In that same spirit, the Marquis de Lafayette took the key of the Bastille in 1789 and sent it to his good friend Washington as a symbol of their common vision of the future.

Their hopes were to be dashed. Sobered by the reign of terror and the revolutionary ugliness from Robespierre and Danton to Napoleon, both Americans and French supporters of the United States revised their views. Gouverneur Morris, for example, the U.S. Ambassador to France, wrote home in disgust: "They want an American Constitution without realizing, they have no Americans to uphold it."

Two hundred years later, that discussion sounds astonishingly fresh. The year 1989 meant it was the French turn for a bicentennial. Yet for all the tricolor celebrations and folderol, there is no mistaking the tale of the two revolutions and how differences in character have led to differences in destiny. The year 1989 also witnessed a critical phase in

I

the powerful birth pangs of democratic freedom around the world, even though in China in June it was terminated by the brutal aborting of the student movement in Tiananmen Square.

Old hopes and fears that the framers' generation would have understood are alive again. Issues that echo those discussed by Washington and Jefferson are in the air—how realistic is it to view democracy as a model set of political arrangements to be exported? What is the role of technology as a force for freedom and democratic change? For democracy to prosper, does a nation have to have certain ideals and assumptions, or is it enough to copy institutions and political arrangements, such as free, recurrent elections, separation of executive and judiciary, and respect for civil liberties?

Opinions differ sharply over the answers to these questions. Just as they do if the questions are raised in a specifically American setting— is the American "new order" universal and for export or is it unique and inimitable? Is the American project fundamentally an experiment and therefore precarious or a destiny and somehow providential? But what seems odd in a century clouded by state repression and sectarian violence is that no part of the American experiment stands out more clearly yet is less appreciated or copied as a key to modern troubles than the religious liberty clauses of the First Amendment. For in the tensions and challenges now surrounding the clauses are some of the deepest and most significant issues of our time. Above all, there is the simple but vital question: how do we, in an age of expanding worldwide pluralism, live with our deepest—that is, our religiously and ideologically intense—differences? In short, what is the relationship today of religious liberty and American democracy?

Tribespeople, Idiots, or Citizens?

Behind this book lie three judgments about the relationship of religion and American public life today: first, that a period of recurring conflict (most notably between 1979 when the Moral Majority was founded and 1989 when it closed its doors) has left the nation with the urgent need to clarify the role of religion in public life; second, that the best way to clarify this relationship lies in reaffirming the place of religious liberty in the common vision of the common good, in accord with the notion of "chartered pluralism" that is outlined here; and third, that the present situation directly confronts Americans with a threefold choice first stated by supporters of democracy in Greece and restated by John Courtney Murray in the early 1960s.

This choice is as follows: as the issues of religion and public life continue to arise, will we respond as "tribespeople," in the sense of those who seek security in a form of tribal solidarity and are intolerant of everything alien to themselves? Or as "idiots," in the original Greek sense of the totally private person who does not subscribe to the public philosophy and is oblivious to the importance of "civility"? Or as "citizens," in the sense of those who recognize their membership in a "commonwealth" and who appreciate the knowledge and skills that underlie the public life of a civilized community?[1]

This volume picks up such questions. It is built on the premise that the democratic experiment in America is based on and is sustained by a vigorous public philosophy and that religious liberty in the past and at present makes an important contribution to its formation. The primary concern of this volume, then, is to specify the nature of that contribution and the philosophical, historical, sociological, and constitutional problems attending it at the end of the twentieth century. But how so?

In chapter 2, William Lee Miller takes stock of the moral project of the American framers. These individuals were audacious in ways that are almost unimaginable today for, in their own minds, they were not just drafting a constitution and a bill of rights but were establishing nothing less than "a new order for the ages." The public philosophy out of which this *novus ordo seclorum* would be conceived was one that saw a nation united and moving forward not on the bases of the brutish competition of material interests alone but upon a commitment to public virtue and civic-mindedness. This conception of public virtue, according to Miller, depended equally on the Puritan ideals of moral commitment and responsibility and Enlightenment ideals of reason and toleration. But it would only flourish where there were assurances of the freedom of conscience and belief.

One might well imagine the framers as misguided utopians except for the fact that their experiment in nation building succeeded. Nevertheless, the framers wrote in a social context fundamentally different

3

from ours. As durable a foundation as they built for succeeding generations, they never could have anticipated the changes and challenges of the late twentieth century.

One of those unanticipated challenges to religious liberty and freedom of conscience was the growth of the modern bureaucratic state. As Harold Berman argues in chapter 3, the state has taken over many of the public responsibilities previously assumed by the churches. In so doing, the state has also acquired the capability of exercising more and more control over the details of people's lives. Another unanticipated challenge, explored in chapter 4 by James Davison Hunter, has come as a result of the expansion of religious and cultural pluralism. At the time of the founding, America was predominantly Protestant in character and in population, while now it embodies a collage of different faiths, and importantly, nonfaith. It is true that the expanding state and an expanding pluralism are institutional changes, but they raise important philosophical questions, not just about the constitutional relationship between church and state but about how to realize the ideals of public justice established by the framers for our own very different circumstances.

In addition to these societal challenges are the problems posed by the inadequacy of assumptions of the prevailing public philosophy. Michael Sandel contends in chapter 5 that modern liberal thought is either deficient or too impoverished to do justice to these problems. Because of its assumption that the state can be neutral and its inability to recognize that many of its citizens are bound to moral ties antecedent to choice, liberalism fails to secure the toleration it promises. The philosophical dilemma is deepened, according to Charles Taylor in chapter 6, because of the sometimes contradictory ways of defining freedom in American political philosophy. Civic freedom (the freedom of self-governance) and liberal freedom (the freedom to live and believe without state or community interference) are sometimes at odds, with opposing social groups in American society pressing one over the other. The genius of the American experiment in the past has been its ability to balance these. Whether it continues to do so in the future or whether a Kulturkampf develops in American society over the priority of one over the other remains to be seen.

The need to reaffirm the principles and structures of religious liberty in this worrisome context is all the more great, according to Peter Berger in the Afterword, because of the twin threats of totalitarianism and fundamentalism (even secular fundamentalism). The reason is that religious liberty undermines the absolutism shared by both the fanatic and the totalitarian. Though the threats posed by these historical developments are surely greater elsewhere in the world, America is by no means immune to either one. For the sake of all human freedoms, religious liberty cannot be taken for granted.

This volume ends with the text of the Williamsburg Charter. This document seeks to articulate a new compact for religious liberty at the end of the twentieth century. By so doing it seeks to articulate solutions to the dilemmas described in the earlier chapters and to reaffirm a commitment to the ideals of the framers' moral project.

Recent Conflicts and Their Context

The proposal for reforging the public philosophy according to the notion of chartered pluralism may be stated as a series of steps in an argument. The first step is to analyze the factors behind the recurring conflicts over religion and public life and assess what they mean for religious liberty and public justice in the future.

The conflicts themselves need no elaboration, though it is helpful to draw a distinction between cases where religion itself is directly the issue and cases where its influence is indirect. Abortion is the principal example of the latter and examples of the former are common—school prayer and New Age meditation, creation science, secular humanism, textbook tailoring, prayer before high school sporting events, Muslim prayer mats in government offices, Gideon's Bibles in hotel rooms, the Ten Commandments on school walls, blasphemy in films and novels, the pledge of allegiance, Mormon polygamy, "Christian nation" resolutions, and so on. For a full generation now the issue of religion and public life has been highly contentious, with an endless series of disputes and the whole subject surrounded by needless ignorance and fruitless controversy, including at the highest levels. Too often, debates have been sharply polarized, controversies dominated by extremes, resolutions sought automatically through litigation, either of the religious liberty clauses set against the other one, and any common view of a better way lost in the din of irreconcilable differences and insistent demands.

At some point, however, the temptation is to take a quick glance at the contestants, apportion the blame, enlist on one side or another, and treat the whole problem as largely political and capable of a political solution. From that perspective, the problem is one that has been created by an ideological clash (the fundamentalists versus the secularists) that overlaps with a constitutional clash (the accommodationists versus the separationists) that overlaps with a psychological clash (the "bitter-enders," who insist on commitment regardless of civility, versus the "betrayers," who insist on civility regardless of commitment) that has produced, in turn, two extremist tendencies (the "removers," who would like to eradicate all religion from public life, versus the "reim-posers," who would like to impose their version of a past or future state of affairs on everyone else)—all this, of course, potently reinforced by technological factors, such as direct mail and its shameless appeals to fear and anger.

Such analyses may be accurate as far as they go. But they stop before they take into account some of the deepest factors, which means they rule out some of the most effective solutions. Of several additional factors, one is especially important to this argument: the recent expansion of pluralism. This is a worldwide phenomenon that links current American tensions to similar trends around the globe. How do we live with our deepest differences? That simple question has been transformed by modernity into one of the world's most pressing dilemmas. On a small planet in a pluralistic age the all too common response has been bigotry, fanaticism, terrorism, and state repression.

Expanding pluralism is no stranger to the American experience. It has always been a major theme in our story, with tolerance generally expanding behind pluralism. But the last generation has witnessed yet another thrust forward in religious pluralism in two significant ways.

First, American pluralism now goes beyond the predominance of Protestant-Catholic-Jewish and includes sizable numbers of almost all the world's great religions (Buddhist and Muslim, in particular). Second, it now goes beyond religion altogether to include a growing number of Americans with no religious preference at all. (In 1962, as in 1952, secularists—or the so-called "religious nones"—were 2 percent of Americans. Today they are between 10 percent and 12 percent.)[2]

The effect of this latest expansion has been to complete the profound sea change initiated by the "new immigration" of the beginning of the century. The United States has shifted from a largely Protestant pluralism to a genuine pluralism that includes people of all faiths and none. The effect can be observed at two different levels in American society. In the first place, the effect of exploding diversity can be seen in the demographic make-up of contemporary American society. The state of California, for example, has America's most diverse as well as its largest population. It now accepts almost one-third of the world's immigration and represents at the close of the century what New York did at the start—the point of entry for millions of new Americans.[3]

California's schools have a "minority majority" in all public school enrollments. Soon after the year 2000 that will be true of the population of California as a whole. (The same situation already exists in all of the nation's twenty-five largest city school systems, and half of the states have public school populations that are more than 25 percent minorities.)[4] The result is a remarkable mix of the diverse cultures of Africa, Asia, Europe, and Latin America. It will also be as challenging a project in culture-blending as New York was in nation building nine decades ago, and Boston was at the birth of the public school movement a century and a half ago.

The effect of the exploding diversity can also be seen in what is a form of cultural breakdown—collapse of the previously accepted understandings of the relationship of religion and public life and the triggering of the culture wars. As a result, a series of bitter, fruitless contentions over religion and politics has erupted, extremes have surfaced, the resort to law court has become almost reflexive, many who decry the problems are equally opposed to solutions to them, and in the ensuing din of charge and countercharge any sense of common vision for the common good has been drowned.

As always with the trends of modernity, the consequences of increased pluralism are neither unique to America nor uniform throughout the world. The disruptive effects can be seen elsewhere in the world, even in totalitarian societies (such as the challenge of the republics to the Soviet Union) and in democratic nations with long traditions of racial and linguistic homogeneity (such as the challenge of new immigrants in Britain).

Nor are the consequences simple. On the one hand, increased plu-

7

ralism deepens old tensions. Under the challenge of "all those others," many are seemingly pressured to believe more weakly in their own faith, to the point of compromise: the more choice and change, the less commitment and continuity. In reaction, however, others tend to believe more strongly, to the point of contempt for the faith of others.

On the other hand, increased pluralism helps develop new trends. Today's dominant tensions are not so much between distinct religions and denominations. As often as not, they are between the more orthodox and the more contemporary within the same denomination (for example, the recent divisions within the Southern Baptist Convention), or between an alliance of the more orthodox in several religions who oppose the more contemporary in those same groups (for example, the pro-life coalition of conservative Protestants, Catholics, Mormons, and so on).

In sum, like it or not, modern pluralism stands squarely as both the child of, and the challenger to, religious liberty—whether because of its presence (given the democratic conditions arising out of the Reformation and the Wars of Religion), its permanence (given the likely continuation of these conditions in the foreseeable future), or its premise (that a single, uniform doctrine of belief can only achieve dominance in a pluralistic society by two means: through persuasion, which is currently unlikely because unfashionable, or through coercion by the oppressive use of state power, which at anytime is both unjust and unworkable).

Not surprisingly, these developments and their logic have hit hard the trio of American institutions that have been so instrumental in tempering the forces of faction and self-interest and helping transform American diversity into a source of richness and strength: the religious liberty clauses of the First Amendment, the public school movement, and the American public philosophy. The upshot is that the public schools have often become the storm center of the controversies, one or other of the twin clauses of the First Amendment have been looked to as the sole arbiter in the partisan conflicts, and the common vision for the common good becomes the loser.

Only when the full extent of this damage and the full range of the causes have been taken into account can any prospective solutions be given realistic consideration.

A Common Vision for the Common Good

The second step in the argument is to clarify what is meant by public philosophy, or common vision of the common good. A defining feature of the United States is that, from the beginning, it has been a nation by intention and by ideas. One of America's greatest achievements and special needs has been to create, out of the mosaic of religious and cultural differences, a common vision for the common good—in the sense of a widely shared, almost universal, agreement on what accords with the common ideals and interests of America and Americans.

Mostly unwritten, often half-conscious, never to be mistaken for unanimity, this common vision has served a vital purpose. It has offset the natural conflict of interests in a pluralistic society, and in particular that impulse toward arbitrariness that is the scourge of totalitarianism and democracy alike. In doing so it has been the binding that maintains unity to balance the richness and pressures of diversity, and it transmits a living heritage to balance the dynamism of progress. Most Americans may never have been conscious of any such thing, let alone the term, public philosophy, but America has always been a working model of one, a public philosophy in action. For Americans, consensus has always been a matter of compact over common ideals as well as compromise over competing interests.

Defined in this way, the notion of public philosophy needs to be distinguished from two similar but different notions. First, this use of public philosophy is different from those who use the term (quite legitimately) to refer to an individual's personal philosophy of public affairs, and thus to the place of public affairs in his or her worldview. In contrast, public philosophy in this book refers expressly to public affirmations shared in common with other citizens. A public philosophy should not only be accessible to others in principle; it is unworthy of the name unless it is actually shared in practice. Second, this use of public philosophy is quite different from civil religion. Like civil religion, public philosophy as used here deals with affirmations held in common. But unlike civil religion, the public philosophy does not require the common affirmations to be regarded as sacred or semi-sacred in themselves. For most Americans, their commitment to the public philosophy is rooted in their own religious beliefs, but the public affirmations are not themselves religious and it is for this reason that they can be held in common with people of other faiths and no faith.

There have undoubtedly been great changes in this concept over time, most noticeably the softening between the harder-edged notion of Puritan covenant and the rather vague midtwentieth century notion of consensus. Equally, the very strength of the notion has sometimes created problems, such as the influence of consensus-thinking on the blind eye turned to cultural diversity and on the countenancing of evils, such as the maltreatment of blacks and native Americans. These are therefore obvious reasons why the subject has recently fallen into disrepute, why its very mention is challenged in some circles, and why there are sometimes competing proposals among proponents of its recovery.

What is certain, however, is that the weakening or disappearance of the public philosophy has definite consequences too, and from Walter Lippmann's critique of public opinion to the current Volcker commission on American public service, a deepening stream of analyses have made this connection and redressed the imbalance. What is also certain is that, because people have different and changing values, the common vision for the common good is never static. It is not in the realm of a final answer. Adjustment and readjustment are an ongoing requirement of American democracy. Since no generation declares, lives, and preserves this common vision in its entirety, there is a need for reaffirmation and renewal in every generation. For Americans to become, in Walter Lippmann's words, "a people who inhabit the land with their bodies without possessing it with their souls" would be a sure step toward disaster.[5]

Consensual agreement over the place of religious liberty in public life is only one component of the wider public philosophy but a vital one. Equally, such a consensus is only one of a trio of agencies (the Constitution, the courts, and the consensus) that are all vital to sustaining religious liberty. But because of the personal importance of faiths to individuals and to communities of faith in America, and the public importance of both to American national life, a common vision of religious liberty in public life is critical to both citizens and the nation. It directly affects personal liberty, civic vitality, and social harmony. Far from lessening the need for a public philosophy today, expanding pluralism increases it. Indeed, for anyone who has reflected on the last generation of conflict over religion and public life, few questions in America are more urgent than a fresh agreement on how we are to deal with our deepest differences in the public sphere.

Chartered Pluralism and Its Contributions

The third step in the argument is to examine the concept of chartered pluralism and its contribution to the current problems. Anyone who appreciates the factors behind the present conflicts is confronted with tough questions. Above all, can there be a resolution to culture wars and a readjustment to the new pluralism without endangering the logic of religious liberty in public life?

At first sight, the search for a just and commonly acceptable solution to these challenges seems as futile as squaring the circle. The questions surrounding the public role of religion in an increasingly pluralistic society appear to form a minefield of controversies, with the resulting ignorance, confusion, and reluctance an understandable outcome. Yet if it is correct to trace the problem to forces such as pluralism as much as to ideologies, individuals, and groups, then there are more victims than villains over this issue, and the wisest approach is to search together for a solution, not for a scapegoat.

In fact, the present stage of the conflict offers a strategic opportunity. Extreme positions and unwelcome consequences are readily identifiable on many sides, and a new desire for consensus is evident. But where and on what grounds could consensus emerge?

The most constructive way forward is to reforge the public philosophy according to a vision of chartered pluralism, such as articulated in the Williamsburg Charter (see the Appendix for the full text). Chartered pluralism is a vision of religious liberty in public life that, across the deep differences of a pluralistic society, forges a substantive agreement, or freely chosen compact, on three things that are the "3 Rs" of religious liberty in a pluralistic society: rights, responsibilities, and respect. The compact affirms, first, that religious liberty, or freedom of conscience, is a fundamental and inalienable right for peoples of all faiths and none; second, that religious liberty is a universal right joined to a universal duty to respect that right for others; and third, that the first principles of religious liberty, combined with the lessons of two hundred years of constitutional experience, require and shape certain practical guidelines by which a robust yet civil discourse may be sustained in a free society that would remain free.

Founded on such a principled pact (spelled out, of course, in far greater depth), the notion of chartered pluralism can be seen to give due weight to the first of its two terms. It is therefore properly a form of *chartered* pluralism, and avoids the respective weaknesses of relativism, interest-group liberalism, or any form of mere "process" and "proceduralism."

But at the same time the agreement is strictly limited in substance and in scope. It does not pretend to include agreement over religious beliefs, political policies, constitutional interpretations, or even the philosophical justifications of the three parts of the compact. Chartered pluralism is an agreement within disagreements over deep differences that make a difference. It therefore gives due weight to the second of its two terms, and it remains a form of chartered *pluralism* that avoids the dangers of majoritarianism, civil religion, or any form of overreaching consensus that is blind or insensitive to small minorities and unpopular communities.

Three features of this compact at the heart of chartered pluralism need to be highlighted indelibly if the compact is to pass muster under the exacting conditions of expanded pluralism. First, the content of the compact does not grow from shared religious beliefs because the recent expansion of pluralism means that we are now beyond the point where that is possible. It grows instead from a common commitment to universal rights, rights that are shared by an overlapping consensus of commitment although grounded and justified differently by the different faiths behind them.[6] Second, the achievement of this compact does not come through the process of a general dilution of beliefs, as happens in the case of civil religion moving from Protestantism to "Judeo-Christian" theism. It comes through the process of a particular concentration of universal rights and mutual responsibilities, within which the deep differences of belief can be negotiated. Third, the fact that religious consensus is now impossible does not mean that moral consensus (for example, "consensual" or "common core" values in public education) is neither important nor attainable. It means, however, that moral consensus must be viewed as a goal, not as a given; something to be achieved through persuasion rather than assumed on the basis of tradition.

Doubtless, further questions are raised by these three points. Do all the different faiths mean the same thing when they affirm common rights? Do all have an adequate philosophical basis for their individual affirmations? Are all such divergences and inadequacies a matter of sheer indifference to the strength and endurance of the compact? Will such a principled pact always be enough in practice, to keep self-interest from breaking out of the harness? The probable answer in each case is no, which is a reminder of both the fragility of the historical achievement of religious liberty for all and the sobering task we face if we would sustain such freedom today. Indeed, the challenge might appear quixotic were it not for the alternatives.

Expressed differently, chartered pluralism owes much to John Courtney Murray's valuable insistence from which the title of this book is taken, that the religious liberty clauses are "articles of peace" rather than "articles of faith."[7] But Murray's distinction must never be widened into a divorce. For one thing, the articles of peace are principled before they are procedural. They derive from articles of faith and cannot be sustained long without them. Civility is not a rhetoric of niceness or a psychology of social adjustment, but discourse shaped by a principled respect for persons and truth. For another, articles of peace should not be understood as leading to unanimity, but to that unity within which diversity can be transformed into richness and disagreement itself into an achievement that betokens strength. In the words of the introduction to the Williamsburg Charter:

> We readily acknowledge our continuing differences. Signing this Charter implies no pretense that we believe the same things or that our differences over policy proposals, legal interpretations and philosophical groundings do not ultimately matter. The truth is not even that what unites us is deeper than what divides us, for differences over belief are the deepest and least easily negotiated of all.
>
> The Charter sets forth a renewed national compact, in the sense of a solemn mutual agreement between parties, on how we

view the place of religion in American life and how we should contend with each other's deepest differences in the public sphere. It is a call to a vision of public life that will allow conflict to lead to consensus, religious commitment to reinforce political civility. In this way, diversity is not a point of weakness but a source of strength.

Understood properly, the concept of chartered pluralism is critical to reforging that aspect of the public philosophy that bears on questions of religion and American public life, especially in the absence of any demonstrable alternative. It is therefore critical to keeping democracy safe for diversity. If it gains acceptance in the three main arenas of conflict—public policy debates, the resort to law, and public education—and if it succeeds in addressing their problems constructively, it could well serve as a public philosophy for the public square, truly a charter for America's third century of constitutional government.

Consequences and Outcomes

The last step in the argument is to set out some of the foreseeable principles and pitfalls that ought to shape prudential judgments as to the best way forward through the controversies.

First, there are three necessary conditions for a constructive solution such as chartered pluralism to be politically successful in achieving justice. Solid concepts and good will are not enough. What is required is intellectual foresight that will anticipate the problem before it becomes full-blown; moral courage that is willing to tackle problems not necessarily considered "problematic" on the current political agenda; and magnanimity that in the present situation will act generously, regardless of its own political position, with regard to the interests of others and especially those of the weaker parties.

Second, there are two unlikely outcomes. These are outcomes that are all but inconceivable and worth stating only because they form the stuff of activist propaganda and counterpropaganda. They are that the conflicts should, on the one hand, degenerate into Belfast-style sectarian violence or, on the other hand, result in an Albanian-style repression of religion, especially in the public square. The combined logic of America's historic commitment to religious liberty and the depth of religious diversity today makes these outcomes virtually impossible.

Third, there are two undesirable outcomes, in the sense of two broad possibilities that might occur should there be no effective resolution of the current conflicts over religion and public life. The milder, shorter-term possibility is that there could be a massive popular revulsion against religion in public life. This could take the form of a-plague-on-both-your-houses reaction to religious contention and therefore lead, ironically, to a sort of naked public square created, not by secularists or extreme separationists, but by a wrongheaded overreaction to an equally wrongheaded religious overreaction.

The more drastic, longer-term possibility is that continuing conflict could lead to the emergence of a two-nation division in American life, with all conservative forces favorable to religion and all progressive forces hostile. A short time ago, such a possibility would probably have been dismissed summarily. But for anyone who appreciates the effects of two-nation divisions on European countries such as France, the implications of the 1988 presidential campaign are sobering. The cultural fissures are worth monitoring.

Fourth, there are two unfortunate outcomes, in the sense of two broad possibilities that might occur even if chartered pluralism succeeds or if current conflicts simply fade away without apparent damage to national life. The first possibility is that, in the generally civil conditions of pluralism, the way is opened for some faith or worldview that would play the game only to win the game and end the game for others (existing candidates from the secular left and the religious right are equally dangerous here).

The second possibility is that, in the same civil conditions of pluralism, civility will itself become so corrupted that, in turn, pluralism is debased into a relativistic indifference to truth and principle. The result would be a slump into apathy, the logic of laissez-faire freedom gone to seed. The outcome would be that corruption of the Republic from within of which the framers warned.

For some Americans, these dangers only confirm the risks of chartered pluralism they feared all along. But mention of the framers is a reminder that the risks are not new. They were built into the experiment from the start. Such risks are the reason why the experiment is open-ended and why the task of defending religious liberty is never finished.

The Williamsburg Charter states, "The Founders knew well that the republic they established represented an audacious gamble against long historical odds. This form of government depends upon ultimate beliefs, for otherwise we have no rights to the rights by which it thrives, yet rejects any official formulation of them. The republic will therefore always remain an 'undecided experiment' that stands or falls by the dynamism of its non-established faiths." As so often, Tocqueville had seen this point earlier and applied it to the two great revolutions of his time. "In a riot, as in a novel," he wrote, "the most difficult part to invent is the end."[8]

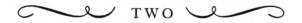

TWO

The Moral Project of the American Founders

WILLIAM LEE MILLER

OTHER NATIONS DO NOT characteristically locate their great nationmaking stories, their norms, their beginnings, their heroes and guides and symbols in so clear-cut and unitary a way in so short and so definite and so recent a period as do the Americans. Usually, for the older nations of the European heritage, the great defining events fade back into the distant past. They come up out of the German forests or down from Olympus or Sinai; they step across the line into the mists of legend and myth. They bring some oracle from Delphi: the nation is founded by the inscrutable action of the gods. The slowly accumulating actions of the many founders spread out across the centuries; there were some Romes before Julius Caesar, and some Romes afterward. There were several Frances before the France, or the multiple Frances, of their Revolution, and these others, their physical contributions more evident in Paris than those of the Revolution, make comebacks. There were Englands before their revolution, and another more glorious Revolution after their revolution, and there was an England before either of them and—in particular—even before the Normans came across the Channel; it seems not only that there will always be, but that there always was, an England.

But for us, this first modern nation, there is no such mist and distance. Our founding heroes line up there pretty squarely, real people, at a rather definite time, between 1763 and 1791, give or take a few years, in places we can still visit, at least in the off season: Philadelphia, Boston, Williamsburg, New York, Concord Green, Valley Forge, and a few other places. We know the names of the founders and can read their copious letters and still try to run the society by the words they put down on sheets of paper.

And what these founders did was not mysterious, equivocal, or opaque, but was filled with a rather straightforward moral and intellectual and—in the good old sense—*political* content. The American founders knew what they were doing, and they said so. Or—they were working out, thinking out, what they were doing, and they were saying so. The United States was to a much greater extent than other nations the product of collaborative human contrivance, of reason and conscience, of deliberation. It might even be said to have been brought into being as a result of moral reasoning; its own beginning might itself be an example of that governance by mutual persuasion that is its own main point.

Of course we Americans exaggerate the newness and the wonderfulness and the element of sheer human concoction in what was done—but, still, it was in some ways new, and it was also in some ways wonderful. It was done by human hands, or rather by human minds, and not by mysterious superhuman powers from another world or inexorable subhuman forces in this one. The United States was brought into being not by an oracle in Delphi but by a committee in Philadelphia.

There was no Solon or Romulus or Moses. There was no single figure who gathered up into his symbolic real or legendary self, by his foundational law giving or glorious deeds, by his connection with divine powers or charismatic leadership, the whole originating and defining action of the people. One might say that the Americans resisted monofounderism (not a word I expect ever to use again) as they did monarchy, on republican principle—the republican principle that was the moral content of their Revolution and of their founding of the states and of the nation.

In particular there was no Caesar. The one candidate for that role, the "father of his country" as he was to be called, overtly and repeatedly rejected it—he formed his "character" (that is, his reputation) in great part out of his rejecting of that role in all its variations. He declined to be king, and he not only declined to be the leader of a military intervention in government, but in a moving moment at Newburgh he stood alone against the restless, angry officers of his army in resisting it. On that consequential occasion George Washington made a serious long speech—something he rarely did—by which the disgruntled officers may not yet have been persuaded, and then, faltering in the effort to read from a letter, fumbled in his pocket to extract his new spectacles, and remarked: "Gentlemen, you must excuse me. I have grown gray in your service and now find myself growing Blind."[1] The officers, much moved, reversed course, voted him thanks, and left quietly. One of Washington's biographers flatly calls this Newburgh meeting of March of 1783 "probably the most important single gathering ever held in the United States."[2] Thomas Jefferson later interpreted what this episode meant: "The moderation and virtue of a single character probably prevented this Revolution from being closed, as most others have been, by a subversion of that liberty it was intended to establish."[3]

This nation did not spring from the brow of some single giant all-purpose progenitor, but rather from a long series of committee meetings. Of careful political reflection before the committee meetings. Of serious reading before political reflection. Of debating societies exploring the reflections. Of arguments in taverns and newspapers. Of committees of correspondence. Of pamphlets answering pamphlets and sermons answering sermons. Of letters—how these people did write letters, serious ones! (How are you; how are the kids; the price of corn is up; the price of pigs is down; now let me tell you what form of government most answers to the needs of human happiness. Twenty pages.) The papers of the major founders march on now volume after volume across the shelves and through the years, loaded with serious letters. In particular this country was argued into existence in a particular kind of committee meeting or debating society that the Americans themselves devised, something new on the face of the globe, the Constitutional Convention chosen by, and reporting to, the whole people.

And then, after the nation was argued into independence and the new governments ratified into existence, there was to be no Napoleon. It is also a point—not to mention invidiously any other nations by name—that the American revolutionaries did not proceed to cut off one another's heads on the glorious guillotine or kill one another in glorious purges (although they were not altogether gentle with the Tories). If they had lived in the age of the photograph it would not have been necessary for the Americans to keep taking the group picture down from the wall to remove somebody from it. It is characteristic of the American founding that its foremost leaders lived through the initial act of defiance, the ensuing war, the peace, the setting up of the states, the shaping of the Constitution, and then the early years of the Republic, furnishing the first four or five (or, if you count the precocious teenager John Quincy Adams who had traveled abroad with his father in the aftermath of the revolution, six) of the nation's presidents. Two of the greatest collaborators from the earliest days of the American Revolution, John Adams and Thomas Jefferson, were able to turn up clear at the other end of things to die with incredible convenience half a century later exactly on the fiftieth anniversary of the Declaration of Independence. Though for a time in the middle of things they had been much opposed to each other, on opposite sides of issues fundamental to the new nation's soul—the Alien and Sedition Acts, for one—they did not lead insurgent forces against each other or banish each other to the hills of Kentucky or kill each other but lived through each other's depredations and settled down in old age to a renewed correspondence—reminiscent, but full of ideas, too, pounding away still on thoughts about government.

Our Founders

The presence of these founders is inherent in the moral understanding of the community of which we are a part—they are part of our social self-understanding. There is a passage in a book by H. Richard Niebuhr in which he uses a great founding American event to illustrate, eventually for religious purposes, the contrast between "inner history," history as lived and loaded with personal meaning, and an external "outer," "objective" history.

First, to prepare the point, he contrasts two different histories of a man who has been blind and who has come to see:

A scientific case history will describe what happened to his optic nerve or to the crystalline lens, what technique the surgeon used or by what medicines a physician wrought the cure, through what stages of recovery the patient passed. An autobiography, on the other hand, may barely mention these things but it will tell what happened to a self that had lived in darkness and now saw again trees and the sunrise, children's faces and the eyes of a friend.

And then Niebuhr contrasts two accounts of the same event in our own American history. The Gettysburg Address, he notes, as the equivalent of the autobiographical account, begins with history: "Four-score and seven years ago our fathers brought forth upon this continent a new nation, conceived in liberty and dedicated to the proposition that all men are created equal." Niebuhr then puts down on the page, as a sufficiently stark contrast, the way the Cambridge Modern History describes the same event:

On July 4, 1776, Congress passed the resolution which made the colonies independent communities, issuing at the same time the well-known Declaration of Independence. If we regard the Dec-laration as the assertion of an abstract political theory, criticism and condemnation are easy. It sets out with a general proposition so vague as to be practically useless. The doctrine of the equality of men, unless it be qualified and conditioned by reference to special circumstance, is either a barren truism or a delusion.

That deflationary Cambridge history might seem to be external his-tory with a vengeance. However that may be, Niebuhr then mentions other examples of the appeal to national memory, to "inner" history— Pericles; Hosea and a Psalmist; Shakespeare on "this sceptered isle"— and adds the observation: "The distinctions between the two types of history cannot be made by applying the value-judgment of true and false but must be made by reference to differences of perspective. There are true and false appeals to memory as well as true and false external descriptions."

It is not, as a positivistic outlook might assume, that the categories of true and false apply only to external history, and that in the realm of value-laden memory anything goes; it is rather that there are other, different, perhaps weightier criteria there, in which the human faculty that is engaged is not simply the objective reason but the loyalty of a remembering self in a community of memory and value.[4] It is in this second way, as part of our inner history, that the founders in particular must be understood.

The Founders' Distance from Us Now

But what values then do these founders, in an American's inner history, embody? The institutions they devised are now for the most part so solidly built into the social order as to be taken for granted. Is there any further connection between these white eighteenth-century colonial males, slaveholders many of them, with their eighteenth-century preoccupations and colonial resentments, and our own vastly different late twentieth-century situation in a mass democracy that is a gigantic world power?

Presumably not many of us today are likely to be country party Whigs, indignant at the "corruption" of the "placemen" of the court party, as these matters were expressed in the prime ministership of Robert Walpole. Although there are American Christians still today, presumably not many would anticipate, with Samuel Adams, the making of the nation into a "Christian Sparta." (It would be uphill work.) Although there are also many Americans who feel themselves to be in the tradition of the Enlightenment, too much has happened between our time and that of Thomas Jefferson for us to look upon the unfolding possibilities of human science, reason, and progress, with the same innocent unalloyed hopefulness that he did.

And it is not easy for us today to work up much indignation at King George III, even with the help of repeated readings, on July fourths, of the long train of abuses the Declaration of Independence set candidly before the world. (The Tories certainly felt there was something inflated and artificial about the high dudgeon into which this rather comfortable group of colonials worked themselves after 1763.) Americans of good heart today, though they may read dutifully about the Stamp Act and the Coercive Acts and the Declaratory Act and the Boston Tea Party, almost certainly will feel much more strongly about another matter, about which our founders seem to have thought, and to have done, very little (and on which what they did do, in the awkward and repugnant compromises of the Constitution, was bad). That other matter of course is this: all of you "patriots" demanding your "liberty," insisting that you won't let the British king make "slaves" of you: what about those persons with black faces who are holding your horses, waiting on your tables, working in your tobacco fields—for them there is an issue of slavery indeed, and of liberty indeed, that goes much beyond a three pence tax on tea.

Or again, Americans today will wonder with Abigail Adams why these men, altogether and only men, gathered in Philadelphia and elsewhere to set candidly before the world the proposition that all men are created equal? And why, in the document proclaiming the universal self-evident truths we hold about human equality, is there reference to "merciless Indian savages"?

Our great-great-great-grandchildren will surely ask similar questions of us—both on matters we can identify (Jefferson and Madison and Washington and George Mason all did know, trembling when they remembered that God is just, that they would one day be called to account about slavery) and also on matters that are not now present to our minds, which our progeny will think should have been. Any reader can make his or her own list of the matters of our present conduct on which we will one day be indicted—those current great issues, perhaps beginning with nuclear weapons, by which we are most disturbed—but none of our lists are likely to include all that those who look back on our time will think they should have included. Our progeny will blame us not only for those things that we have done that we ought not to have done, and those things that we have left undone that we ought to have done, but also for those things that are not even present to our consciousness so that we can include them in the confession. And the defense attorneys for our ghosts will respond then the way the founders respond now: you others living in that distant world of another age do not understand the realities, the limitations of ours. The founders' defenders can say that any generation that does as well with its given situation, its possibilities, as the founders did with theirs will do very well indeed. In contemplating these matters, historical awareness, an attention to the limitations that encircle a period, is necessary to consider fairly the actions and the achievements of people within that time.

So if they were "creatures of their time," what if anything remains of the moral outlook of the founders, as distinguished from the continuing institutions they created, that has any bearing on us today?

Public Thinkers

The founders' bearing on us today includes the fact that they were simultaneously public thinkers and public actors. Their thinking and acting contained what we must today call—in order to make clear the element of value in it—a "moral" aspect.

It has been written that "the great debate over liberty and order which took place in America from 1763 to 1789 was also a debate about the nature of man."[5] It has also been written that in the two decades prior to the meeting of the Constitutional Convention, "American political discourse was an ongoing public forum on the meaning of liberty."[6] It has been written, further, that "America, in the era when democratic thought was being formulated, conducted one of the most informed public debates on the nature of free institutions ever to grace the annals of any nation."[7] It could still further have been written, perhaps it has been, that in those years the Americans conducted a great clinic or seminar on the nature and purposes of government. (One could read the most famous paragraph in *Federalist 51* as having said that.)

In the American colonies in the late eighteenth century there was an extraordinary outpouring of discussion about all those interconnected questions: human nature, government, liberty, order, the foundations of human institutions. The principles on which human society rests were examined clear to the bottom. The examination was, however, not an exercise in speculation only but an integral aspect of the making of an actual state. Adams wrote to a friend a sentence, often quoted, remarking on the great, and very rare, opportunity that they and others of their generation shared:

> You and I, my dear friend, have been sent into life at a time when the greatest lawgivers of antiquity would have wished to live. How few of the human race have ever enjoyed an opportunity of making an election of government for themselves or their children! When, before the present epoch, had three millions of

people full power and a fair opportunity to form and establish the wisest and happiest government that human wisdom can contrive?[8]

Here is a scene that can serve as an epitome. One evening in January 1776, just as opinion among the American colonials is taking the big step from protest to Revolutionary War, a learned man from Williamsburg, Virginia, named George Wythe, who among many other things had been Thomas Jefferson's law teacher at the college of William and Mary, paid a visit to a lawyer-politician from Braintree, Massachusetts, named John Adams, in Adams's chambers. The two men discuss the great current topic. Adams described the event as follows:

> In the course of conversation upon the necessity of independence, Mr. Wythe, observing that the greatest obstacle in the way of a declaration of it was the difficulty of agreeing upon a government for our future regulation, I replied that each colony should form a government for itself, as a free and independent State.
>
> "Well," said Mr. Wythe, "what plan would you institute or advise for any one of the States?"
>
> My answer was, "It is a thing I have not thought much of, but I will give you the first ideas that occur to me": and I went on to explain to him off-hand in short-hand my first thoughts.
>
> Mr. Wythe appeared to think more of them than I did and requested me to put down in writing what I had then said, I agreed and, accordingly, that night and the next morning wrote it and sent it in a letter to him.[9]

This letter of John Adams, which came to be printed by the initiative of others, contained much of what Adams would elsewhere defend, in particular about so-called balanced government, in his drafting of the constitution for the newly independent state of Massachusetts four years later, and in his three-volume *Defense of the American Constitutions*, written in London while Adams was the first United States minister to Great Britain ten years later.

One more example, from a later moment. In the spring of 1786, and again in the spring of 1787, a young Virginian named James Madison, Jr., undertook what has been called "probably the most fruitful piece of scholarly research ever carried out by an American."[10] This was his study of the constitutions of ancient and modern republics, and then of the "vices" of the political system of the United States. That study shaped James Madison's own ideas, which shaped the so-called Virginia Plan, which shaped the U.S. Constitution, which shaped the new nation's institutions, which shape the public life of Americans and through them the world today. So Jemmy Madison, undertaking his research in Orange County, Virginia, and in New York in the important year of 1786–87, boning up for the big exam time in Philadelphia in the summer, was engaged in no small endeavor.

Among the six greatest founders, four—Thomas Jefferson, James Madison, Alexander Hamilton, and John Adams—were self-starting intellectual workers in this political-moral field, reading and writing and thinking things through. The other two, George Washington and Benjamin Franklin, the oldest and the most celebrated in the founding period, and the two in the group who had not gone to college, aided and abetted these thinkers in many important ways.

An American public thinker who stands in a tradition with the founders—one of the few of whom that may be said in the twentieth century—John Dewey, wrote this about the founders:

> We may as well be amazed, as well as grateful, at the spectacle of the intellectual and moral calibre of the men who took a hand in shaping the American political tradition. The military and moral, although not especially the intellectual, repute of Washington has made him a part of the common heritage. There are also Jefferson, Hamilton, Madison, followed at some distance by Franklin and John Adams, and at a greater distance by Monroe. There were giants in those days.

The door of history broke open, the usual human inertia and passivity about received social arrangements was for a moment overcome, and these human beings could see daylight by which to rearrange the institutions under and through which they lived. They were offered by history the opportunity to examine and reform human institutions fundamentally; and they took the opportunity.

There was, in all that founding thought and argument, an element of disinterestedness, of objectivity, and of service to a lasting public good. It goes against the grain of a modern sensibility to admit that this might be so—to grant that some people somewhere someday might be able to act or think to some degree in a way not strictly dictated by their own interests—but was it not so? Take only the example of the founders enclosed in what we are repeatedly told was a hot room in Philadelphia. Of course there were small-state and large-state factions, and nationalists and localists, and protectors of local interests, notably slavery, and men of lesser as well as greater stature. Nevertheless, one cannot read any of the several accounts of that proceeding without being impressed by the serious intention to serve the long term and common good that moved above and through these disputes—indeed, the long term and common good not only of this Republic, but of republicanism in human history.

The Oracle of Truth

The American political system is the product, to an unusual degree, of such serious, informed, collaborative, and disinterested brainwork. It needs to be emphasized—because Americans have fallen so far from honoring, or practicing, these human goods—how much these founders were readers, writers, and thinkers. Many of them—products of Princeton, Harvard, Yale, William and Mary, King's College, private tutoring by Anglican clergymen—were able to call up, with whatever accuracy, classical references and analogies.[11] They referred to—often it seems stole from—the best contemporary political philosophizing. They engaged in extended close reasoning (as, for example, in *The Federalist*). And they put this work of the intellect at the service of the country they were bringing into being.

They undertook this work of thinking not as might an "ingenious theorist" planning a constitution "in his closet or his imagination" (as Publius—James Madison—was disdainfully to put it in *Federalist 37*) but with the awareness that what they thought and said would make a difference in an actual society. Moreover, they were, in addition to being (some of them) intellectuals, experienced politicians. In their time the men of thought and the men of action had not yet been separated; these men could be both. The Americans were not thinkers isolated from practice and from action—they were, indeed, inclined to dismiss speculative theory not tested by experience—but men who served in the Continental Congresses and state assemblies, ran for office, debated the forming of legislation, and served as governors, ministers of state, and cabinet secretaries. Many of them had fought in the Revolutionary War. This active and practical experience enriched their thinking, and their reading and thought in turn deepened and guided their practice.

The "twelve who ruled"—the Committee of Public Safety—in the year of terror in the French Revolution, were very different from any comparable group among the Americans. They were "intellectuals" in the modern, pejorative sense, with absolutistic ideas unqualified by the give-and-take of actual local politics. Moreover, for an American, the ideas of these Frenchmen came from unfortunate sources, in which there was little political realism: too much Rousseau, as Americans might see the matter, and too little of the more qualified Anglo-American Puritan-Protestant heritage.[12] The result, in the most extreme leaders of the terror—Robespierre and, even more, St. Just—was a stunning cloture of mind and absence of habitual, salutary self-criticism. That the American founders stood, and still do stand, for a contrasting politics in the inner history not only of Americans but of "republicans" or "democrats" around the world is suggested— among a host of other places—by the recent remarks of Adam Michnic, an interesting thinker in the Polish Solidarity movement. Michnic wrote about their twentieth-century Polish protest movement: "I pray that we do not change from prisoners into prison guards" and that "we suspected by using force to storm the bastilles of old we shall unwittingly build new ones," sentences loaded with meaning in the history of revolutions since these first modern ones in the late eighteenth century. And in the same spirit and to the same point Michnic wrote that Solidarity never had a vision of an ideal society: "It wants to live and let live. Its ideals are closer to the American Revolution than to the French."[13]

Madison, in *Federalist 37*, behind his mask as Publius, praised in anonymity the Philadelphia convention of which he was a member and contrasted its work, carried out under the pressure of reality, with that of a mere "ingenious theorist" in his closet. And in *Federalist 14*, he answered those who said that the proposed Constitution is a novelty never heard of in the political world, nor found in any of the great theorists of the past:

> But why is the experiment of an extended republic to be rejected merely because it may comprise what is new? Is it not the glory of the people of America that, while they have paid a decent regard to the opinions of former times and other nations, they have not suffered a blind veneration for antiquity, for custom, or for names, to overrule the suggestions of their own good sense, the knowledge of their own situation, and the lessons of their own experience?

But what Madison is describing, and what he himself eminently represented, was not some recourse to raw thoughtless, bookless practice or "experience" in place of political thinking but exactly political thinking as it should be. The error in the one direction—"blind veneration"—is to drop the great names and books and references, the tag lines and themes—Aristotle, Machiavelli, Locke, Montesquieu—without at all doing what Aristotle, Locke, Machiavelli, and Montesquieu did—to think. The error in the opposite direction is to speak out of one's own immediacy without that training and guidance, without that cumulation of the thinking of many others, to reason with and against. The founders were practical, experienced, and open to novelty. That should not be allowed to obscure the point that they read and thought deeply.

The American founders thought about society and government and politics and the nature of humankind, which may not have been the subjects the English metaphysical poet Thomas Traherne had in mind when he wrote this line, but which perhaps we can apply to our forefathers: "He who thinks well serves God in His inmost Court."

A New Order for the Ages

The founders served God in His inmost court—not perhaps the way they would have put it—by thinking out the governmental institutions under which we still live, in a vastly different country in a vastly different world more than two hundred years after their time.

They read and thought and argued. They sought in their arguing to shape a nation in accord with, and as a bearer of, ancient ideals of liberty, and, for some of those inclined to more sweeping claims, of universal "sacred and undeniable" or "self-evident" truths. The new nation they brought forth upon this continent was such that it could later plausibly be said to have been conceived in liberty and dedicated to the proposition that all men are created equal. To a quite unusual degree, in other words, the founding of the United States was a moral project, a venture in bringing into being a worthy answer to the ancient problem of living together in an organized society.

They were not exactly modest about what they were doing. On the nation's great seal the American patriots described what they were building as *novus ordo seclorum*—a new order of the ages. (An American reader can find that phrase today on the back of the dollar bill.) The new order was not, however, expected to be completed, final, or perfect. The framers produced a Constitution, the product of compromise, pluralism, and realism, by which it may almost be said none of them were satisfied.

The founders were not utopians; the limitations of the language with which we deal with these matters perhaps requires us to call them realists, although it is important to distinguish this use from modern uses of that word that indicate a realpolitik that is very close to cynicism. The American founders were not cynics. They were not yet perhaps "pragmatists" or "meliorists," but they certainly knew that what they built would change and grow—should change and grow. James Madison, not given ordinarily to the coining of good phrases, did say that this new land would be the "Workshop of Liberty."

There was something still of the Puritans in this moral project, building the frame of a commonwealth in accord with a universal moral order. But there was also something of the new secular outlook, of the Enlightenment, in that the founders discovered that political-moral order not by consulting and interpreting authoritative texts but by their examination of "experience"—their own, but as we have said, also and much more important, the experience of other peoples and of past ages, the experience of the human race as one could read about it in the book of history. Key founders, in the atmosphere of the Enlightenment, did believe that there were certain universal rules about human conduct, and about the shape of governments, which if you would read carefully and widely and think clearly you could discover, and on those truths you could build something that approached the ideal and that would last.

But the project partook of something that was emerging from the new spirit of science—of Jefferson's heroes, Locke, Bacon, and Newton—also in this regard, that it left the future open. Although on the one side the founders sought grounding in universals, in a way that the relativized mind of the twentieth century might not do, on the other side they did not expect their product to be complete or final; they left it general and they left it open, for much to be filled in later.

Exemplars and Shapers of Republicanism

The founders sought to shape a nation in all its particularity, but at the same time they sought to do this in accord with, and as a bearer of, universal "self-evident" truths. They were thinking out a moral-political position on the great question of the good society. They were doing that thinking in conscious participation in the long history of the polity that goes by the name of republic. The American founders had their own symbolic collective memory, their own inner history, although less neatly located than the one they have provided for us. The founders saw themselves standing in the long tradition of "republics" and of liberty that reached from the classical ages through many adventures in the history of Europe, that would be no doubt quite vulnerable when explored by objective scientific historians but which nevertheless was for them the bearer of value and guide for action.

The only ideological or philosophical claim in the federal Constitution they wrote was to guarantee to every state in these United States a "republican" form of government. The founders may not have agreed precisely about what that term republic meant, but there were certain kinds of polity that it excluded (monarchies, aristocracies, tyrannies—not so irrelevant to our time and even our country as you might at first think, if you think of the principles underlying those rejections) and certain positive meanings within those boundaries. Madison in *Feder-*

alist 14 and again in *Federalist 39* explains what republican principles are, in order to test the new Constitution against them.

The founders brought forward with new clarity the ancient republican ideal of a whole people governing itself by its own moral discourse. They gave that ideal new life and lasting power exactly by a radical alteration in the understanding of the conditions under which, and the institutions through which, such an ideal could be realized. They gave that ideal a realistic base, in institutional checks and in application to a large and expanding nation. In order to carry out their complicated task they sought solid grounding in the universal characteristics of humankind.

The founders came to be resolved—and of course this was the great novel achievement—to show in theory and in practice that republican principles did not require a small city-state but that they could be realized—realized better—in a large territory and society, a "compound" or "extended" republic. They were resolved, further, that the institutions conformable to those desiderata should also not fall apart, should be stable, should last—as indeed they have. Also—as Madison explains in the attractive *Federalist 37,* in which he discusses, behind the veil of anonymity, as though from outside, the complexities the Philadelphia convention faced—they should have Hamilton's great desideratum, energy. The founders sought this difficult combination: a republican government—and a stable government. And an energetic government. A republican government—with built-in protections against the instability and weakness of republics. Protections—which themselves are compatible with republicanism.

They were conscious that their effort had significance going beyond this nation—not to be small about it, had significance for the world. James Madison the note taker reported James Madison the delegate as having said, on June 26 at the Constitutional Convention: "He [that is, Madison] observed that it is more than probable we were now digesting a plan which in its operation would decide for ever the fate of Republican Government." [14] George Washington would say in his inaugural address that "the Sacred fire of liberty and the destiny of the republican model of government were deeply and irrevocably staked on the experiment now undertaken by the American people." [15] And the greatest interpreter of the founders would explain more than four score years later in a cemetery in Pennsylvania that what happened to this Republic was a test to see whether this nation or any nation so conceived and so dedicated should perish from the earth.

Fortunate Compound

Did the founders' idea of republicanism assume and require a groundwork in "virtue"—public virtue, civic virtue—and was that virtue to be supplied by religion? The answer to this question must be mixed. Some members of the founding generation were aligned in one way and some in another. New England Congregational preachers interpreting the Revolution to their congregations in the thought world of Covenant theology differed from South Carolina slaveholding plantation owners interpreting it in terms of their own privileges, and both of these differed from New York Dutch patroons and Philadelphia Quaker businessmen. Although the Americans of the late eighteenth century were by close or distant affiliation overwhelmingly Protestant of the Reformed tradition, and in major part from the British Isles, they were nevertheless sufficiently diversified already to reinforce the principles of toleration with the facts of pluralism. There were not only the English and—an important addition—the Scotch-Irish, but also Germans, Dutch, French, and others, including the many continental sects that found a refuge particularly in Pennsylvania. The thirteen colonies stretching from New Hampshire to Georgia for 1,500 miles were variegated not only in geography, climate, population, and economic base but also to some extent in national origin and in religious and intellectual background.

The atmosphere in 1787, after the bracing, disillusioning, and illuminating experience of life under the new state constitutions and under the ineffectual Articles of Confederation, was not the same as the heady idealistic revolutionary atmosphere of 1776. The atmosphere on either of those dates, when the preoccupation was politics, was not the same as the atmosphere in 1740, during the Great Awakening, when the preoccupation was religion. In the first flush of independence many thought and hoped the new American republics would be something like the classical republics, or even like the "Christian Sparta" of Sam Adams: cohesive communities in which "public virtue"—a shared willingness to sacrifice personal interest to the public good—would prevail; the experience under the new state constitutions in the 1780s began to suggest that the long-term picture would be more complicated. There was a great sense of the importance of the kind of public spirit that the founders indicated by their phrase—taken over from ancient and modern writings about republicanism—public virtue, and it occurred not only in New England but also in Virginia and elsewhere; but there was also a certain amount even then of do-your-own-thing individualism. In New England especially, although not only there, these first Americans did insist that "piety and virtue" went together and together were the necessary foundation of a republic; the enormously important Massachusetts constitution of 1780, very largely the work of John Adams, a model for the federal Constitution in many ways, included specific provision for tax support for teachers of piety and morality—preachers in the Congregational churches were what the early Americans mostly had in mind—in order to provide that essential foundation in religion and morality that a republic required. But the most eminent representative of the Enlightenment in the new United States, Thomas Jefferson, held as a central tenet exactly that religion and morality could be separated: that virtue did not require the underpinning of religion, and indeed that it was weak and misleading to think that it did.

All of this is to say that the founders differed as we do, although not as widely. It is important to give such a mixed answer to the question about religion and the nation's founding because late twentieth-century Americans, riven with conscious and unconscious partisanship on these issues, make tendentious interpretations of the sort one wants to avoid—of the sort that run straight through the late twentieth-century debate about "church and state," which debate, in and out of the courts, and on all sides, seems to be marked by nothing whatever but advocacy, invective, and polemic. Because the founders are important symbols of national values, citizens of a later time twist them in order to align those revered figures with their own convictions.

The religious version of this partisanship is familiar and obvious and was for a long time dominant. Early in the nineteenth century there came in the new nation a triumph of a kind of evangelical Protestantism. In that new atmosphere of the nineteenth century there came a Parson Weemsing of the founders that has been repeated in times of popular religious revival since, very much including the present time. When the editors of the George Washington papers tell about all the requests they get for quotations establishing Washington's religious piety—from, among others, White House speechwriters—they roll their eyes heavenward. There is an understandable impulse on the part of the pious segment of the American populace to get its two pieties lined up: Bible and Constitution, disciples and founders, God and country. But it leads to a distorted and misleading picture of our national past. And that distortion is more consequential than others, because the founding has mythic and narrative power for Americans: it is our shared memory, which, as I have said, has claims on us all.

In the long run, across the whole culture, that interpretation cannot prevail—the interpretation, that is, that insists upon religion as the necessary foundation of America's republican institutions. The Enlightenment, with its edge of skepticism, was too much present in the Revolution, in the new nation's institutions, in key founders, in the mind of significant segments of the people—and, in effect, in the great silences and protections and negations of the Constitution itself—for that to be persuasive. So was the principle of liberty, derived partly from Christian sources but partly from other sources. If many Christians of the sorts that predominated in the American colonies came to believe in free institutions, and if the origins of such institutions can in some part be found in the Puritan Revolution, and in the longer Christian heritage, it is nevertheless doubtful that the Christian tradition alone would ever have generated, from within itself, a fully articulated free society, a new republic, a "democracy." Republicanism, and the Enlightenment—to some degree outside the Christian tradition—were necessary for that result. The United States had the great good fortune to be born not only out of the intersection and combination of republicanism and Christianity but also to be born in that springtime of the modern world.

And those great silences, negations, and protections of the Constitution stood there preventing any closed and final "religious" interpretation of the nation's essence—any interpretation, that is, that would shut the door on the "free thinkers" who fled to this country in hope, on "infidels" or "secular humanists," who found in "democracy" their faith, on the various forms of unbelief, and quasi belief, and amiable indifference, that this nation spawned and sometimes even welcomed. When one hears imperialistic claims about the place of religion in the foundation of America's political institutions one needs to be reminded again not only of the diversity of the colonies but also of the role in the American founding of the Enlightenment, of deism, of a certain skepticism about and emancipation from religious preoccupations in the late eighteenth century, precisely in the instruments of the American founding.

On the other hand when the modern day heirs of the Enlightenment (if such they be) who occupy many of the seats of power and influence and scholarship and intellectual leadership in twentieth-century America, reject or more often just assume away any serious role of religious belief in the formation of the United States—that needs to be qualified, too. The United States was not simply the outcome of religious belief, but such belief was important. Three successive powerful movements lie in the background of the making of America: the Protestant Reformation, and especially that large branch of it called the Reformed tradition (which is more than "Calvinism"); Puritanism in England, out of which came the most intellectually and spiritually cohesive and energetic of the settlers in the New World; and the "Great Awakening," the national conversion, by which the culture of the new nation was to be affected. Whereas later believers look back at the founding through the screen of the evangelical revivals and of their own sympathies to find more piety than there was in early America, the cultured among the despisers look back through the screen of their unbelief to find only Thomas Jefferson and Tom Paine and more unabashed secularism than there really was.

The successive waves of American intelligentsia keep expecting religion to have vanished; or they write as though it has already done so, and then are continually surprised that it has not. Each of the awakenings, or ages of religious revival, catches them in attitudes of grumpy denial and surprise . . . including the revival, such as it may be, of the bicentennial period in which this is written. They write whole histories of American life and spirit that skimp the religious element in the imagination of the American people; they say, about religious affirmations, "nobody believes that anymore." One is reminded of the statement that Yogi Berra is said to have made about a well-known restaurant: "Nobody goes there anymore. It's too crowded."

The distinctive, and perhaps also normative, feature of the American beginning was neither the religious underpinnings nor the emancipation from them but the combination. And as the Christian religion and republicanism, streams coming down out of the past, intersect and affect each other, yet another kind of movement, not arising in the ancient past but defined by its time, cut across them both, at right angles as it were, and affected them both: the Enlightenment. Although these three movements, Christianity, republicanism, and the Enlightenment, were often separated and even opposed to one another, as they join to form the United States, they interpenetrate, qualify, and in some measure endorse one another. At least they are not as sharply hostile to one another as they are elsewhere. Although the Christian religion in Europe was often, and often seen to be, the great opponent of the modern age—of liberalism, of republicanism—in the United States it was no opponent but a friend. The Americans, unlike the Europeans, explicitly disentangled themselves from monarchy, explicitly repudiated aristocracy and hierarchy, implicitly repudiated priesthood, and set in their place a new nation with liberty and equality at the center without casting the Christian religion as any kind of opponent. Whereas the French revolutionaries would institute a new calendar, beginning with the first year of the republic, the American revolutionaries, although omitting any religion from their Constitution, nevertheless, when they got to the signing, dated it "in the Year of our Lord, 1787."

One consequence from these fortunate beginnings was that the United States would not divide politically, systematically, along a religious faultline. As John Courtney Murray, the leading American Catholic thinker of the twentieth century, would observe, there were not to be two Americas, as there are two Frances, two Italys, and two Spains.[16]

In the United States religious conservatives were not antirepublican, and the political radicals were not necessarily antireligious. As to the conservatives, one may say that the American nation left the deep European religio-political conservatism behind three times: when the reformers broke with the Catholic Church; when the Puritans left En-

37

gland; and when the Americans declared independence. With this last event the Tories, the Loyalists, went back to England, or they went to Nova Scotia or elsewhere in Canada, in very large numbers; this component that, despite many fleeings and murderings, continues to exist in other countries of Christendom, does not exist in the United States—that is, a religio-political conservatism that has some connection with the ancient regimes.

As to the "radicals," although major leaders of the American founding can be said to have been a part of, or much influenced by, the Enlightenment—Thomas Jefferson, Benjamin Franklin, perhaps Jefferson's friend James Madison, and even the New Englander who was also a Puritan in many ways, John Adams—these American Enlightenment revolutionaries did not regard hanging the last king in the entrails of the last priest as part of their revolutionary program. Although an American leader, Thomas Jefferson, could regard the Revolution as a repudiation of the rule of kings, priests, and nobles, the kings, priests, and nobles to be repudiated were all conveniently elsewhere. Although the Revolution, in the atmosphere of the international Enlightenment, did generate a "religion of reason," a "republican religion," repudiating orthodoxy, which had a certain popular following, and some well-known leaders like Ethan Allen, the hero of Ticonderoga, and Joel Barlow, the Connecticut wit, and Elihu Palmer, who published a journal called *The Temple of Reason,* the partisans of this republican religion, having fought side-by-side in the Revolutionary War and in subsequent political battles with New Light Baptists, old-style Presbyterians, Anglican gentlemen, Dutch-reformed New Yorkers, standing order Congregationalists, German Lutherans, found themselves after the battles over the French Revolution with a diminishing following. Although many wagons going west took with them a copy of Tom Paine's *Age of Reason,* a great many more wagons, no doubt, carried a copy of the Bible. And that energetic book salesman Parson Weems, who endorsed the one and disapproved of the other, nevertheless represented the American spirit in enterprise, as well as in moralism, and sold both.

Of course one would not exactly want to propose Parson Weems as an exemplar of the genius of the American founding. Not on most points. But there is something to be said for that inclusiveness. We would do well to emulate it today. It is exactly from the fortunate mingling, and not from the exclusive contribution of any one of the parties, that certain distinctive merits of this remarkable nation arose. That is the way we may see it to have been in our national origins, and that is the way we may see it ideally to be today: that the several parties may become less threats to and rejections of one another than complements to and correctives of one another. As that implicit and largely inadvertent collaboration between a Puritan-Protestant movement, and other religious movements, and the Enlightenment, and secular republican movements, worked together (without any of them exactly intending to) to create the foundation of this nation, so we should attempt to mold the same fortunate pluralism, among a much wider spread of parties to the great conversation in the contemporary United States. One might even say that was the essence of the moral project of the American founders.

THREE

Religious Freedom and the Challenge of the Modern State

HAROLD J. BERMAN

I F WE ARE TO UNDERTAKE what the Williamsburg Charter calls "a fresh consideration of religious liberty in our time, and of the place of the First Amendment religious liberty clauses in our national life," we must ask, first, what religion meant in America when the Bill of Rights was framed, and what its relationship was to government; and second, how both religion and government have changed in the course of time, especially in the last two generations. It is only on this broad background of historical development that the free exercise and the establishment clauses of the First Amendment can be interpreted and applied in a way that is true both to the text of the Constitution and to the future of the nation.

Although the First Amendment is usually said to provide for the separation of church and state, in fact it does not contain the word "church" but speaks instead of "religion"; and it does not contain the word "state" but speaks instead of "Congress." Moreover, in the extensive public discussions that were carried on in the late eighteenth and early nineteenth centuries concerning the religious liberty clauses of both the federal and the state constitutions, reference was rarely made to relations between church and state; debate centered, rather, on the extent to which "religion" and "government" should be free from each other's control. This indeed was James Madison's own terminology.[1] Despite Thomas Jefferson's famous remark that the First Amendment erected "a wall of separation between church and state," it is important

The assistance of Leonard J. Vaughn on this chapter is gratefully acknowledged.

to recognize that in America at that time there was no state in the sense in which that word is used in classical Western political theory; nor was there then (nor is there now) a "church," either in the sense of a single universal ecclesiastical entity such as the Roman Catholic Church, which maintained an autonomy vis-à-vis the various secular polities of Europe in the eleventh to sixteenth centuries, or in the sense of the established churches that existed in the various kingdoms of Europe after the Protestant Reformation. As John Noonan has eloquently stated,

> "Church and State" [is] a profoundly misleading rubric. The title triply misleads. It suggests that there is a single church. But in America there are myriad ways in which religious belief is organized. It suggests that there is a single state. But in America there is the federal government, fifty state governments, myriad municipalities, and a division of power among executive, legislative, administrative, and judicial entities, each of whom embodies state power. Worst of all, "Church and State" suggests that there are two distinct bodies set apart from each other in contrast if not in conflict. But everywhere neither churches nor states exist except as they are incorporated in actual individuals. These individuals are believers and unbelievers, citizens and officials. In one aspect of their activities, if they are religious, they usually form churches. In another aspect they form governments. Religious and governmental bodies not only coexist but overlap. The same persons, much of the time, are both believers and wielders of power.[2]

The framers of the American federal and state constitutions were keenly aware of the historical experience that is implicit in the phrase "church and state." They chose at the federal level, and eventually in all the states as well, a new and different solution, namely, the right of all persons, both individually and in groups, to exercise their religion free of restraint by government, and also the duty of government to exercise its powers and functions without identification with religion. But the fact that religion and government were to be free of each other's control was not understood to exclude their reciprocal influence on

41

each other. Officeholders, as Noonan indicates, were not expected to shed their religious commitments at the door of the office.

In considering what was meant by religion and what was meant by government when the federal and state constitutions were adopted, and what is meant by religion and government today, one should have in mind not only the various kinds of beliefs that may properly be called religious, and not only the various kinds of speech and worship associated with those beliefs, but also their manifestation in social action. Today religion is often defined solely in terms of personal faith and collective worship. Such a definition neglects the repercussions of such faith and worship in social life. In the Puritan theology that prevailed in America throughout the eighteenth century,[3] often in association with both Anglican and "free church" traditions, religion was understood not only in terms of a covenant of grace but also in terms of a covenant of works.[4] A person's relationship to God was understood to involve his active participation in the life of the community. More than that, religion was understood to be not only a matter of personal faith and personal morality but also a matter of collective responsibility and collective identity.

In seeking the meaning of the religious liberty clauses of the First Amendment, I propose, first, to focus attention on the role that religion played in the social life of America in the eighteenth and nineteenth centuries. To do so is to be faithful to Madison's conception that religion comprises not only "the duty which we owe to our Creator" but also "the manner of discharging" that duty.[5] For Madison, as for Americans generally in the 1780s and 1790s, and indeed for generations thereafter, free exercise of religion included freedom of religious groups to take an active part in regulating family responsibilities, education, health care, poor relief, and various other aspects of social life that were considered to have a significant moral dimension.

Conversely, the concept of government that prevailed when the federal Constitution and the first state constitutions were adopted, and that continued to prevail for generations thereafter, was that government's role in the regulation of family responsibilities, education, health care, poor relief, and other similar matters of social welfare, as distinct from political and economic concerns, is not a direct but an indirect one, namely, to help maintain conditions in which the carrying on of such activities by religious associations, or associations inspired by religious motivation, can flourish.

Yet the prevailing social roles and functions of religion and government in the United States today are quite different. The contrast between the earlier situation and the present situation is obvious enough. In the 1780s religion played a primary role in social life, as I have defined that phrase, and government played a relatively minor, though necessary, supportive role, whereas in the 1980s religion plays a relatively minor, though necessary, supportive role and government plays a primary role. On the other hand, the role played by government in the social life of America in the 1780s (and for almost a century and a half thereafter) was openly and strongly influenced and directed by religion, whereas in the 1980s that is much less true and in many respects not true at all, while the role played by religion in the social life of America in the 1980s is openly and strongly influenced and directed by government.

To put this last point in strong terms, and perhaps with some exaggeration: whereas two centuries ago, in matters of social life that have a significant moral dimension, government was the handmaid of religion, today religion—in its social responsibilities, as contrasted with personal faith and collective worship—is the handmaid of government.

Lest this be misunderstood as a plea for a return to some golden age, it should be emphasized that what is described here is the irrevocable transition of twentieth-century America from a nation that had previously identified itself as Protestant Christian to a nation of plural religions, including not only many varieties of Protestants, Catholics, Jews, and Muslims but also diverse other groups whose belief systems, though nontheistic, have much of the character and many of the functions of religion. Most of these theistic and nontheistic belief systems have come to be defined largely in terms of personal life rather than in terms *both* of personal life *and* of social, or public, or civic responsibilities.

Thus the first two parts of the chapter will address two paradoxes in which America now finds itself by virtue of (a) having a constitutional text that, when it was adopted, presupposed the active role of religion, on the one hand, and the relative passivity of government, on the other,

43

in various realms of social life, and (b) living now in a time when, on the one hand, religion is becoming increasingly privatized, and, on the other hand, its public, or civic, or social functions are being increasingly swallowed up by—what now by reason of that very fact may properly be called—the secular state.

The third and concluding part of the chapter will consider the significance of this shift in the social roles of religion and government for our understanding of how the religious liberty clauses of the First Amendment should be interpreted and applied.

Religion and Government Past

In sketching the social role of religion in America in the late eighteenth and early nineteenth centuries, it will be useful to specify its role in a number of areas of social life.

First, take family life. In the late eighteenth century and, indeed, for some generations thereafter, the family in America was widely thought to be not only a civil but also a religious unit. Births, marriages, deaths, and other family events were often recorded in family Bibles. Family prayers were not uncommon. Attendance at church was generally by families, with seating in family pews. Marriage was subject to ritual and law derived from church traditions. As late as 1917 the United States Supreme Court spoke of marriage as a "holy estate."[6] A leading treatise on family law published in 1899 stated that marriage is a "state of existence ordained by the Creator," "a consummation of the Divine command 'to multiply and replenish the earth,'" and "the only stable substructure of social, civil, and religious institutions."[7] Bigamy, polygamy, incest, and homosexuality were punishable offenses. Betrothals were required to be formal and marriages were required to be contracted with parental consent and before witnesses. Divorce laws in the various states were derived from English ecclesiastical law, which was itself derived partly from the canon law of the Roman Catholic Church and partly from Protestant religious norms. Couples who sought divorce had to publish their intentions and to prove in court adequate cause or fault.[8]

Following English precedents, American statutes and court decisions in the late eighteenth and early nineteenth centuries gave the husband and father the dominant role in family life. He had the primary right to control the person and residence of his wife and children. Indeed, the wife could not sue or be sued except with her husband. In case of separation or divorce of the spouses, the father was given preference in the custody of children. These legal rules favoring male domination were identified to a large extent with religious tradition, including traditional interpretations of the Bible.

In the realm of education the pattern was similar. In 1787, and for many decades thereafter, education in the home was widespread and outside the home it was largely in the hands of the churches and of private teachers, of whom a considerable percentage were clergymen. Education at all levels had a strong religious purpose and character. There was little public education, although three of the thirteen original states provided for it in their constitutions. In most states, most education was provided by the dominant churches, such as the Congregationalist church in Massachusetts and other parts of New England and the Episcopal and Presbyterian churches in Virginia.

It was only in the 1820s and 1830s that the education of the youth came gradually to be a responsibility of government. Even then, however, this responsibility was conceived to be fundamentally religious in character. That is apparent from the speeches and writings of the great apostle of the public school, Horace Mann, who continually emphasized that only through public education could a Christian social consciousness and a Christian morality be inculcated in the population as a whole.[9]

Horace Mann did not invent these views. As early as 1787 it was stated in the Northwest Ordinance that "religion, morality, and knowledge being necessary to good government and the happiness of mankind, schools and the means of education shall forever be encouraged."[10]

As the number of religious sects and the prevalence of public schooling increased in the first half of the nineteenth century, state support of specific, doctrinal education dwindled. At the same time schools did not lose their more generally Christian aspect. Prayer and reading from the Protestant Bible, usually at the beginning of the day, set a religious tone to instruction. Though some states passed laws requiring Bible reading most states did not bother to legislate established

45

custom. "Even Thomas Jefferson, though questioning the value of religious education for children, insisted only that in the public schools of Virginia, 'no religious reading, instruction or exercise, shall be prescribed or practiced, inconsistent with the tenets of any religious sect or denomination.'" [11]

Not only the public elementary and secondary schools but also state colleges and universities were intended to promote Christian education. The University of North Carolina, which opened in 1795, had as its president during most of the first third of the nineteenth century a Presbyterian minister who, with strong support from the state legislature, "insisted on regular attendance by students at religious worship and on orthodox religious instruction." [12] Of the 246 colleges and universities founded in America before 1860 the great majority were denominational foundations; most of the others were founded by union of several churches; only seventeen were state institutions, and even these considered themselves Christian and required students to attend religious services. [13]

Much of the same can be said of social welfare. Poor relief was primarily a responsibility of religious groups in many parts of the United States during the late eighteenth and early nineteenth centuries. In Virginia, for example, the parishes regularly provided money and food to parishioners who were in need. Also the vestry of the parish would levy tithes on the parishioners to reimburse members of the parish for support of aged paupers, orphan children, and indigent parents, as well as to maintain a workhouse and poor farm. [14]

In the northern states the townships took responsibility for poor relief, but this was under the strong influence of Puritan conceptions and with active participation of the churches. In general, those who were willing to work but had fallen on hard times were to be helped, but those who were "idle or vicious" were to be punished. [15]

Philadelphia was a pioneer in establishing a secular system of public poor relief, administered by city officials who assessed and collected a poor tax. Nevertheless, the need for private charity remained a pressing one and the various religious denominations maintained parallel systems of relief for their own adherents. The public and the private systems worked together. Thus in combating successive epidemics of yellow fever in the late 1700s and early 1800s, Philadelphia physicians, ministers, and merchants cooperated in administering both public and private funds. Moreover, public and private relief of disease and of poverty was combined with "reclamation" and "uplift" of the "idle or vicious" poor onto the path of industry and morality.[16]

In comparison with the role of religion, the role of government in social life in 1787 and thereafter was very limited. Though it was indeed a responsibility of government to regulate family life, through laws on marriage and divorce, parental powers, and the like, government regulation of these matters took the form of implementing religious norms and concepts. If we use the language of "church and state," we may say that family law, which had once been in the province of canon law and ecclesiastical courts, was in the American Republic a part of secular law administered by secular courts. But if we use the language of "religion and government," we must say something rather different, namely, that family law, though administered by government, remained essentially religious in character and, more specifically, Protestant Christian.

Similarly, much of the criminal law, enacted and enforced by agencies of government, embodied religious concepts. Not only did the legislative, executive, and judicial branches of government prohibit, prosecute, and punish such religious crimes as blasphemy, Sabbath breaking, sexual deviation, gambling, and dueling, but also the entire concept of crime and punishment was rooted in religious doctrines of sin and penance.

In 1787 religion played a guiding role, and government an implementing role, in family law and criminal law. With respect to education the role of government was even more restricted. Government-sponsored education was in its infancy. When it did begin to flourish a generation later, the guiding role of religion was paramount and the role of government was, once again, an auxiliary one.

With regard to poor relief, health care, and other forms of social welfare, the role of government at all levels, local as well as state and federal, was minimal. These were matters left almost entirely to voluntary associations, especially religiously motivated associations.

It would be a mistake to attribute the limited role of government in social welfare to a laissez-faire theory of the state. It is not true that the founders of the American Republic conceived the role of government to be that of a "night-watchman," with the duty solely to police the operation of a free-market, individualistic society. Especially in the economic sphere, government at all levels was thought to have an important positive role to play. But in *social* life, in the sense in which I have employed that term, including, to be sure, the economic function of poor relief, the role of government was minimal, compared with what it has become in the twentieth century—and the role of religion was maximal.

Specifically, government was thought to have an auxiliary role, an implementing role, and religion was thought to have a directing role, a motivating role. This relationship was symbolized dramatically in the sermons that were preached at the opening of legislative sessions at the state level as well as at other state occasions.[17] Sometimes lasting two hours or more, such sermons emphasized the Christian covenant of works between God and man as well as the mission of public servants to maintain civic virtue.

That government had the function of implementing goals set by religion is evident in the large amount of governmental support given to religion, and especially to religious education, even at the federal level. The general language of the Northwest Ordinance has already been quoted in that connection; more specifically, the Northwest Ordinance provided for government establishment of religious schools.[18] The Ohio Company was given a huge grant of land with specification that a substantial acreage be used "for the support of religion."[19] The federal government provided a Roman Catholic school for the Indians of the Northwest Territory (the bill was signed by President Thomas Jefferson)[20] and subsequently sent missionaries to Indians (this was upheld by the Supreme Court in *Worcester* v. *Georgia*, 1832, with an opinion by Chief Justice Marshall).[21] Congress gave a land grant in 1832 to a Baptist university and in 1833 to Georgetown College (in what is now Washington, D.C.), which was a Jesuit college for educating Roman Catholic boys. At the state levels widespread governmental aid to religious activities continued into the twentieth century.[22]

Religion and Government Present

In the twentieth century, we see a complete reversal of the respective roles of religion and government in American social life. Defined in terms of their social functions, these two have radically changed their meaning.

It is unnecessary to introduce data to prove that government today is largely responsible for education at the primary and secondary level and plays a major role in higher education as well. Public education today is almost wholly secularized—not only in the sense that it is operated by government but in the sense that government, and not religion, sets its goals.

Similarly, health care is no longer primarily a religious or even a charitable concern. It is primarily a political, a governmental concern. Although it is aided by charitable contributions to medical services, its standards and goals are set to a considerable extent by government. Where religion enters the hospital, chiefly in the form of chaplains' services, it does so in an auxiliary and private capacity.

Relief of poverty is also, above all, a governmental concern. Religion makes an important contribution, but it is (once again) essentially an auxiliary contribution. Church shelters for the homeless are an excellent example: the relationship of the churches to the people whom they shelter is largely an impersonal one. These are not, as they would have been in 1787, their own parishioners. Moreover, homelessness in America today is a large-scale problem that can only be solved ultimately by government-aided housing and mental hospital programs, and in recent years the churches, among other voluntary agencies, have stepped in chiefly to help meet a crisis that arose when government aid was reduced. Similarly, churches have given government substantial assistance in administering foreign aid in various countries—operating under essentially political guidelines. [23]

Perhaps the most important reversal in the roles of religion and government is in family life. The urban family today is not, for the most part, a religious unit. Family law no longer reflects religious beliefs. The organization of the family—or rather the disorganization of the family—is now treated in practice as a problem to be regulated primarily by governmental rather than by religious norms. The economic and legal aspects of family life are treated independently of its spiritual aspects.

The same is true of urban crime. Criminal law has been almost wholly divorced from sin and penance. With some important exceptions, religion today has little to do with defining what is criminal or with punishment or other treatment of criminal offenders.

In short, religion has lost most of its importance as a way of addressing publicly the major social problems of our society. It has become increasingly a matter of the private relationship between the believer and God. Worship remains collective, and the churches continue to play an important part in the individual lives and the interpersonal relations of their members; but the occasional gatherings of fellow worshippers make only a minor contribution toward solving society's social needs.

As religion has become increasingly a private matter, the social responsibilities of government have become magnified. Society has become increasingly identified with government. Divorced from religion, government has become increasingly political, so that the words government and politics, or government and state, have become almost synonymous. The state, as the great Polish Nobel Prize winning poet Czeslaw Milosz has said, threatens to swallow up the civil society.[24]

The Implications of the Reversal

How does, how should, this change in the roles of religion and government—indeed, this *exchange* of roles—affect our understanding of the religious liberty clauses of the First Amendment? Must one draw the conclusion that the very words "religion" and "government" (or more exactly "Congress") in the First Amendment—and in parallel provisions of the state constitutions—have come to have fundamentally different meanings today from what they had not only in the 1780s and 1790s but also in the following century and a half? If that is true, does it follow that the "original intent" of the framers of the religious liberty clauses is irrelevant to the interpretation of the words themselves?

The difficulty of interpretation remains acute if we look not to the intent of the framers as such but rather, as the leading framer himself recommended, to the intent of the people of the several states who ratified it.[25] That avoids the tortuous path of committee drafts, legislative debate, and contemporary polemics. Yet the broader question is equally intractable: how is the word "religion," as it was understood in 1787 or 1791 by a nation whose electorate was divided largely among

Anglo-Saxon Protestant Christian denominations, to be interpreted for a nation whose electorate is divided not only among Protestants, Catholics, Jews, and Muslims, all theists, but also among many other non-theistic religious groups as well as agnostics and atheists, and then cross-divided not only among whites and nonwhites but also among numerous ethnic subdivisions of both whites and nonwhites?

Should we then disregard the historical dimension of the Constitution and attribute to the term "religion" in the First Amendment the meaning that it has in current usage? This, indeed, is what the courts have done when they have said that religion is the private affair of each individual, a matter of his or her personal choice, rather than a matter of the collective identity of a nation made up of religiously diverse communities.[26] On the basis of a purely individualist definition of religion, the theory of a constitutional "wall of separation between church and state" might indeed be justified. The definition, however, is open to challenge. It remains for churches, synagogues, and other religious communities to demonstrate that religion does have a social dimension and that creative ways can be found to bring religion and government together.

If religious communities can, in fact, show that not only private belief but also social commitment is an integral part of what they mean by "religion," then the courts should begin to expand the free exercise clause of the First Amendment; and if the social commitment of various religious groups is exercised in cooperation with government programs in ways that do not adversely affect other religious or non-religious groups, then the courts should begin to contract the no establishment clause, thus reconciling the two clauses. In the words of the Williamsburg Charter, "In the light of the First Amendment, the government should stand in relation to the churches, synagogues and other communities of faith as the guarantor of freedom." That freedom should include not only the freedom to exercise inner belief but also the freedom to exercise social commitments intrinsically involved in such belief.

Such a reconciliation of the two clauses could also serve as a basis for reconciling twentieth-century constitutional law with the constitutional law of the eighteenth and nineteenth centuries.

There are already many examples of constitutionally permitted cooperation between religion and government. One need not confine one-self to traditional examples such as government employment of chaplains in the armed forces and in legislatures, ceremonial prayers at the opening of legislative and judicial sessions, the pledge of allegiance to the flag, and the language of official patriotic songs. At least equally important examples are those of cooperation between churches and government agencies in the building of low-cost housing and in other forms of poor relief, as well as in the treatment of alcoholism and drug addiction, in foreign aid, and in various other governmental activities that have a strong moral dimension. There can be no constitutional objection, surely, to the use of religious counselors by courts in resolving questions of family responsibility in cases of divorce and care of children.

Even in the acute question of "religion in the schools," there are ample opportunities with the Constitution for reciprocal aid by government to religion and by religion to government. Public schools may offer courses in the history of religion, in the Bible as literature, and in comparative religion. Public school teachers at all levels are free to explain Jewish beliefs relating to Chanukah and Christian beliefs relating to Christmas. Such instruction does aid religion without, however, constituting an establishment. Blatant discrimination against one or more belief systems might indeed rise to the level of a constitutionally prohibited preference of the majority faiths. Yet it is hard to imagine that conflicts among religions, as well as conflicts between theistic religions and various forms of so-called secular humanism, could not be presented in a classroom setting openly and fairly to all sides.

Similarly, the widespread use of government funds—especially at the municipal and state levels—to finance social welfare activities in which religious groups participate does indeed "aid" not only religion in general but also those religious groups in particular. Such aid should be, and for the most part is, understood, however, not as an establishment of religion but as part of government's responsibility to protect the free exercise of religion.

America today is groping for a public philosophy that will look beyond our pluralism to the common convictions that underlie our pluralism. It must come to grips with the fact that freedom of belief—which includes freedom of disbelief—rests, in the last analysis, on the foundation of belief, not on the foundation of skepticism. That is what John Adams meant when he said that the Constitution, with its guarantee of freedom to believe or disbelieve, "was made only for a moral and religious people. It will be wholly inadequate to any other."[27] It is not to be regarded as an instrument framed (in the words of a Missouri court in 1854) for a society "composed of strangers . . . each with a religion of his own, bound by no previous social ties, nor sympathizing in any common reminiscences of the past."[28]

At the same time, our public philosophy must also come to grips with the deep conflict in our society between orthodox religious belief systems and widespread indifference or opposition to such belief systems. We have in the past sought to resolve this conflict largely by trying to sweep it under the rug. We have pretended that all belief, both religious and nonreligious, is the private affair of each individual. This has inhibited the articulation of a public philosophy grounded in our fundamental beliefs concerning human nature, human destiny, and the sources and limits of human knowledge.

Especially with regard to debate concerning the religious liberty clauses of the First Amendment, there should be open discussion of the significance of its historical roots. More particularly, a reconsideration of Adams's and Madison's conception that religious freedom can only be secure if it is undergirded by religious faith[29] could lead to a reinterpretation of the relationship between the no establishment clause and the free exercise clause—a reinterpretation that would permit not only "religion" to cooperate with "government" but "government" openly to cooperate with "religion"—without discrimination for or against any belief system (and hence without establishment) and without coercion (and hence without restriction upon free exercise).

FOUR

Religious Freedom and the Challenge of Modern Pluralism

JAMES DAVISON HUNTER

THE MORAL PROJECT of the founders was to construct not only a constitutional order but a public philosophy that would establish broad and equitable standards of public justice, standards that would sustain this new nation long after those whose genius established it had died, indeed, for many generations into the future. Surely this high purpose was at the heart of the religious liberty clauses of the First Amendment. In the sixteen words that make up the two clauses, there would be a firm guarantee that as long as the nation existed, the convictions of conscience could exist free of state interference and coercion. So too, there would be the guarantee that the interests of particular faiths would not be extended by the direct or indirect patronage of the state, at least not to the disadvantage of minority faiths.

Though established as general principles of law that could incorporate a broad range of faiths in the world of eighteenth- and early nineteenth-century America, the practical intention of the clauses could have only been to reduce the deep and longstanding tensions spawned by the various inter-Protestant rivalries. Take, for example, the Congregationalists and Unitarians in Massachusetts, Connecticut, and New Hampshire against the "swamp of sectarianism" spreading in Pennsylvania and other mid-Atlantic states; the Methodists, Baptists, and Presbyterians in the southern states against one another and against the power of the Episcopalians; the Campbellites, Stoneites, and the Disciples on the western frontier against the theological and spiritual complacencies of more established denominations in the East; and the "Old Lights" against the "New Lights" in several denominations.

These rivalries—born of the conviction that each denomination and faction possessed the true legacy of the Reformation while all others were at least partially mistaken—defined the prominent cultural tensions of that time and therefore the tensions that needed to be resolved most urgently. In this context, the clauses were relatively effective; their moral purpose was largely realized.

In principle, of course, the clauses also provided the mechanism for resolving conflicts outside of the world of Reformational Christianity, and in particular, between Protestants and Catholics and between Christians and Jews. But at the time, these conflicts were minor for the simple reason that, by the start of the nineteenth century, Catholics comprised only 1 percent of the population and Jews and free-thinkers even less. Both in population and character America was indisputably Protestant.

Yet the potency of the clauses to establish an even broader foundation of public justice—one that would incorporate the interests of a growing non-Protestant population—was soon to be tested. The challenge came with the massive immigration of Catholics from Ireland and Germany between the 1830s and the 1850s, the immigration of German (Ashkenazim) Jews later in the century, and the growth of the new American sect of Mormonism. But even with this expansion of religious and cultural pluralism, the liberties guaranteed by the First Amendment did not, for all practical purposes, extend far beyond the Protestant world. While no one Protestant denomination enjoyed the patronage of the state, the cause of a "pan-Protestantism" had a substantial, if unofficial, government endorsement. The consequence was the restriction of the full religious liberties of other, non-Protestant communities of belief.

The struggle of minority faiths in the nineteenth century to achieve in practice what had already been guaranteed in principle by the First Amendment was often bitter because the resistance of the Protestant establishment was deep and sometimes violent. This was especially true for the Catholic community that, because of its remarkable demographic growth, provided the first and most credible threat to Protestant domination over public culture. The conflict, of course, was more than theological in nature. In the Protestant-Catholic conflict, as in the Protestant conflict with Mormons and Jews, the antagonism centered over the competing social, political, and economic interests of each community of faith in what was, in effect, a zero-sum cultural contest. The larger Protestant community sought to maintain if not extend its control over the symbolic territory of public life against the intensifying claims of the Catholic, Jewish, and Mormon communities for their own space in the public square. As is well known, the most intense and visible struggles came in the attempt of minority faiths (and especially the Catholic Church) to establish a recognized and protected presence in electoral politics and in public education. By the beginning of the twentieth century, the ideals of the First Amendment religion clauses (as they extended to Catholics and Jews) had still not been fully realized, as the chronicle of anti-Catholicism and anti-Semitism unhappily documents.

The failure to fully realize the ideals of the First Amendment in the nineteenth century is significant because it provides something of a precedent for developments occurring today. Certainly many of the social dynamics taking place in the present find a parallel in the past. How? In the last half of the twentieth century, the power of the clauses to establish public justice has been challenged again by the further expansion of religious and cultural pluralism in America. Catholics now constitute about 28.0 percent of the population; Jews about 2.5 percent. Mormons now compose 1.6 percent of the population (roughly 3.8 million people) and are one of the fastest growing religious denominations in America. Much more significant, of course, is the expansion of pluralism beyond the traditions of Judeo-Christian faith. The number of Muslims in America, for example, is about the same as it is for Mormons. (Indeed, there are more Muslims today than there are Episcopalians!) The number of Hindus and Buddhists has also grown prodigiously since the end of World War II. But far more significant is the growth of that part of the population that social scientists call secularists—those who claim no religious preference at all. The secularist camp represents the fastest growing community of "moral conviction" in America. Between 1952 and 1962 secularists made up only 2 percent of the population. By 1972 secularists composed 5 percent of the population. By 1982 they reached 8 percent and by the end of the decade, they made up approximately 11 percent of the population.[1]

Another factor is worth considering in this light as well. Pluralism has expanded in terms of the number of faiths or cultural traditions, but it has also expanded within traditions. All of the major religious traditions are now divided (minimally) into orthodox and progressive camps. Certainly the dominant factions in Protestantism, Catholicism, and Judaism are all characterized by an embrace of the secular Enlightenment. With some exceptions the survey evidence makes clear that these liberal religious traditions share much more in common culturally with one another and with the growing secularist population than they do with those orthodox believers in their own religious heritage.[2]

It would be difficult to overemphasize the novelty of contemporary cultural circumstances vis-à-vis those that prevailed in the late eighteenth century when the Bill of Rights was drafted. Arguably, these new circumstances have created even greater challenges to the moral purpose of the First Amendment than those posed by the increasing prominence of Catholicism, Judaism, and Mormonism a century ago. This is so in a particular way. As the portion of the "secularist" and liberal religious population has grown, so too has an awareness of the secularistic nature of contemporary American public culture. Some on the religious right, of course, claim that there is a conspiracy afoot, that "secular humanists" and their ideological allies now "control" the major institutions of American life. While no serious scholar would accept that assessment at face value, most recognize the secular character of public life and the fact that there is a growing constituency who favor these circumstances. Based on mountains of empirical evidence, drawing from the work of Max Weber, Emile Durkheim, and Robert Bellah, one could argue quite plausibly that a secularistic humanism has become the dominant moral ideology of American public culture and now plays much the same role as the pan-Protestant ideology played in the nineteenth century.

A host of profound questions has been raised by the recent expansion of pluralism. But this essay examines one that goes to the heart of jurisprudence and public philosophy and has played a characteristically acrimonious part in recent public policy debates: given the expansion of pluralism, and especially of secularism, how are we to define "religion" and how are such definitions to serve the traditional ideal of

57

public justice? These questions have loomed in the background of many recent debates, yet they have not been answered directly. There have been too many prior matters to resolve, the chief among them in this instance being how to legally treat nontheistic faiths and ideologies. Though not religions in the same sense that Protestantism, Catholicism, and Judaism are considered to be, should they be considered religions for First Amendment purposes? If so, how does this affect the legal interpretation of the religious liberty clauses?

A Problem of Definitions

The courts themselves have been groping toward the answers to these questions for several decades. As with so many other legal issues, this issue has also become entangled in technical debate, with discussion focusing upon how the word "religion" is to be defined for First Amendment purposes. Should religion be defined by substantive criteria, that is, by the "meaning contents of the phenomenon"?[3] Or should religion be defined by functional criteria, by what it does for individuals and communities?[4] These two approaches to definition are by no means mutually exclusive, though both carry different analytical consequences.[5] The substantive model generally delimits religion to the range of traditional theisms: Judaism, Christianity, Islam, Hinduism, and so on. The functional model, in contrast, is more inclusive. By defining religion according to its social function, the functional model treats religion largely as synonymous with such terms as cultural system, belief system, meaning system, moral order, ideology, world view, and cosmology.

For all practical purposes, even those who prefer the functional definition still think of religion in its traditional sense—a body of beliefs and practices emanating from a transcendent, often supernatural source. But as the approach implies, the functional model focuses on a cultural system and does not require a deity for the system to be considered religious in character. Confucianism and Theraveda Buddhism, for example, contain no supernatural reference to speak of, yet few would exclude them from the pantheon of world religions. Other examples are less obvious, such as political ideologies, social movements, and therapeutic techniques. Scholars typically refer to these as "quasi religions" or "religion-surrogates" or "functional equivalents" of religion.[6]

It should be stressed that both methods for defining religion are rooted in venerable intellectual traditions in the social sciences,[7] and no resolution has been reached. So it is hardly surprising that there has been ambivalence over which approach to adopt for legal purposes. A review of how religion has been defined in American jurisprudence will help frame the contemporary dilemma.

Defining Religion in the Courts

The Supreme Court first referred to the nature of religion and the First Amendment in the 1870s.[8] At a time, in other words, when the Protestant consensus was still strong. From then until well into the twentieth century the courts defined religion in strictly substantive terms— religion referred to theistic notions of divinity, morality, and worship.[9] In 1890, for example, the justices held that "the term 'religion' has reference to one's view of his relations to his Creator, and to the obligations they impose of reverence for his being and character, and of obedience to his will."[10]

The reason for adopting this restricted approach was simple. As Justice David Brewer wrote for the majority opinion in *Church of the Holy Trinity* v. *United States* (in 1892), "Our civilization and our institutions are emphatically Christian. . . . From the discovery of this continent to the present hour, there is a single voice making this affirmation . . . that this is a Christian nation."[11] Thus it was entirely understandable that in the cases dealing with the legality of Mormon polygamy, the justices would legitimate their decision of opposition by referencing "the general consent of the Christian world in modern times."[12]

Forty years later, the courts again relied on the strict substantive approach. In *United States* v. *Macintosh,* a Canadian immigrant and professor at the Yale Divinity School was denied citizenship because he refused to bear arms unless he first was allowed to decide if the war was "morally justified." In its decision, the Supreme Court maintained that "the essence of religion is belief in a relation to God involving duties superior to those arising from any human relation. . . . One

59

cannot speak of religious liberty, with proper appreciation of its essential and historic significance, without assuming the existence of a belief in supreme allegiance to the will of God."[13] Although the Court implied that any religion was inherently theistic, it discarded earlier notions of an American Christian nation.

Not long after this decision, however, the challenge of modern conditions found courts beginning to expand their definition of religion to include its function. Significantly, all of the cases turned on free exercise and involved constitutional rights. The first indication came in the early 1940s when a federal court of appeals heard a case involving a conscientious objector. Mathias Kauten sought exemption from military service because he maintained that such service would be in violation of his "religious conscience." The legal difficulty posed by his argument was that he openly admitted that his objection was not rooted in a "belief in a deity." Nevertheless the court ruled in Kauten's favor, in part through a broadened definition of religion. As the court put it,

> Religious belief arises from a sense of the inadequacy of reason as a means of relating the individual to his fellow men and to his universe—a sense common to men in the most primitive and the most highly civilized societies. . . . It is a belief finding expression in a conscience which categorically requires the believer to disregard elementary self-interest and to accept martyrdom in preference to transgressing its tenets. . . . Conscientious objection may justly be regarded as a response of the individual to an inward mentor, call it conscience or God, that is for many persons at the present time *the equivalent of what has always been thought a religious impulse.*[14]

The significance of the decision was that it altered the central reference point in the legal understanding of religion. Where the reference point had previously been the nature of belief (in a divine being), it was now the psychological function of belief. The Supreme Court affirmed this position not much later when it argued that courts could not consider the truth of particular creeds or tenets, only the sincerity with which individuals adhered to their creed.[15]

The shift toward a functional definition of religion was affirmed yet again in the early 1960s. In 1961 the Supreme Court struck down an old Maryland statute requiring all public employees to declare their belief in God. *Torcaso* v. *Watkins* involved a citizen seeking to become a notary public who was unwilling to make the declaration because it violated his freedom of belief. The Court agreed, stating that the Maryland law had also violated the no establishment clause of the First Amendment because it put "the power and authority of the State of Maryland . . . on the side of one particular sort of believers—those who are willing to say they believe 'in the existence of God.' "[16] It further maintained that "neither a State nor the Federal Government can constitutionally . . . aid all religions as against non-believers, and neither can aid those religions based on a belief in the existence of God as against those religions founded on different beliefs."[17] Of those "religions founded on different beliefs," it explicitly mentioned both the Eastern religious faiths of Buddhism and Taoism, as well as the functional equivalents, ethical culture and secular humanism.

In 1965 the Supreme Court again affirmed the functional approach in another case involving conscientious objectors. Until then the Selective Service Act of 1948 granted exemptions only to objectors whose religion was directly related to their belief in a Supreme Being. But in 1965 the Court concluded that the words "belief in a Supreme Being" could be construed as a "belief that is sincere and meaningful [and] occupies a place in the life of its possessor parallel to that filled· by the orthodox belief in God of one who clearly qualifies for the exemption."[18] In the majority opinion, the Court referred to Paul Tillich's definition of religion not as a belief in God so much as an "ultimate concern"; that which individuals consider to be at the heart of their lives, what they take seriously without reservation. The justices concluded that religion could be defined to include all sincere beliefs "based upon a power or being, or upon a faith, to which all else is subordinate or upon which all else is ultimately dependent."[19]

This series of decisions expanded the constitutional definition of religion in a way that paralleled the expanding pluralism of American religion. Their chief effect was to include nontheistic and, in particular, secularistic ideologies under the protection provided by the religious liberty clauses. On the surface the justification was both obvious and unassuming. The framers of the Bill of Rights had not anticipated an America in which religious faith (and nonfaith) was so diversified, and where that diversity was so prominent. Therefore the courts were simply making constitutional adjustments that would serve the interests of public justice under new conditions.

To that point, the functional definition of religion had been applied almost exclusively by supporters of nontheistic religions claiming their rights under the free exercise clause. It had not been applied to the no establishment clause by their opponents as it would be later in the Alabama textbook case, *Smith* v. *Board of Education.*

A Question of Interests

Legal definitions are not merely a matter of academic curiosity or intellectual concern. They are linked directly to the interests of all sides of a debate. The courts' recognition of a broader functional definition of religion in the early 1960s was clearly framed with an eye to the claims and interests of the nontheists. This new definition of religion guaranteed rights that had not previously or (at least formally) been recognized. These court decisions represented a significant achievement for humanist organizations and intellectuals who had been working for nearly three decades to have humanism recognized as a nontheistic religion or at least as a functional equivalent of a religion.[20] At the same time, if the recognized rights of free exercise were not balanced by the matching requirements of no establishment, the functional definition was bound to appear counter to the interests of the orthodox (and the evangelicals in particular), because secularism could challenge and even replace Protestantism's de facto favored status in American law, education, and cultural mythology.

As mentioned, the application of the "functional test" to the establishment cases was not determined in the early cases. But, obviously, different interests would be served by the different possible outcomes. In no establishment cases the interests are precisely opposite to what they are in the free exercise cases. A functional definition of religion in no establishment cases would include humanism as a religion, and thus would serve the interests of the religiously orthodox (and public justice), because it would ensure that secularistic values and ideals never be favored by the state over transcendent values and ideals. Conversely, a substantive definition of religion would serve ideologically progressive and secular interests because, being excluded from no establishment prohibitions, secular and similar ideologies could be supported by the state and not be challenged legally.

Yet the significance and subtleties of this issue are still not fully appreciated. Despite the fact that the Supreme Court has recognized nontheistic faiths as "religions" for free exercise purposes, the argument that secular humanism is a religion remains implausible for most intellectuals. Indeed, common wisdom asserts that secular humanism is purely a myth invented by the religious right—a convenient scapegoat designed by lunatic conservatives. But the question still remains: are naturalistic beliefs such as secular humanism "religious" in any sociologically meaningful sense? If so, how is one to make sense of them in light of the requirements of the no establishment clause?

Is Secular Humanism a Religion?

The last two decades have witnessed the growth of a more aggressive and openly secular variety of humanism, partly in response to the general expansion of secularism and partly as a deliberate reaction to fundamentalist insistence that all humanism is secular humanism. (In fact, "naturalistic" or "scientific" humanism was originally the smaller strand of nontheistic humanism in America.)

Within the logic of the social sciences, the status of secular humanism can be explored at two levels.[21] There is little doubt that, *as a formal movement*, secular humanism serves as a meaning system or a cosmology. It is designed to provide individuals not only with a clear, alternate means of making sense of their everyday lives but a mechanism for legitimating the larger social order as well. To its adherents, it is a functional equivalent of religion. Seen this way, secular humanism is one part of the wider movement of humanism that is institutionalized in such organizations as the American Humanist Association, the Council for Democratic and Secular Humanism, the Unitarian Universalist Association,[22] the Fellowship of Religious Humanists, the American Ethical Union, the United Secularists of America, the Washington Ethical Society, and the Association for Humanistic Psychology.[23] The "creeds" of the wider movement, which include state-

63

ments about the nature of the universe, the nature and origin of knowledge and of values, of the origins and goals of human life, are set out in such documents as the *Humanist Manifesto I* (1933), the *Humanist Manifesto II* (1973), and *A Secular Humanist Declaration* (1980) (among many others).[24] And its interests are articulated by such periodicals as *Free Inquiry, The Humanist,* and the *Progressive World.*[25]

It is important to stress that the earlier, and originally larger, strand of this humanist movement has been quite open about its religious dimensions and regards itself as an avowedly religious humanism. This explains why there are humanist "churches" known publicly as churches.[26] These churches carry 501 (c) (3) tax status with the Internal Revenue Service, exempting them as religious organizations from the requirement to pay taxes. Further, they have credentialed "ministers" (in the Ethical Culture Society, they are called leaders); in the AHA—which was founded mainly by religious humanists—they are called humanist counselors and act as their "ordained ministry" and, in fact, "enjoy the legal status of ordained pastors, priests, and rabbis."[27] These churches have Sunday services (in the Ethical Culture Society, these are called platform meetings), Sunday schools, and rituals (including weddings, naming ceremonies, memorial services, and the like).

Such groups make up a large part of the network of organizations at the heart of the popular humanist movement in America.[28] Using sociological criteria, then, it is not difficult to make the argument that as a popular movement humanism can be seen as a religion or quasi religion. It is certainly no less religious than say, Transcendental Meditation, EST, Psychosynthesis, Arica Training, Scientology, or any of the other organizations of the human potential movement. And humanism is perhaps no less religious than ethical Confucianism or the "high road" tradition of Buddhism.

To make this argument is to invite further speculation about the 'type of religion' humanism might be. At this level it could be understood as both a predecessor and a variant of the larger and more diverse human potential movement. Humanism became established organizationally decades before the proliferation of religious and quasi-religious experimentation of the mid- to late 1970s, but it has evolved into one organization among many human potential groups. Although movement humanism was and is primarily ethical and philosophical in concern whereas most of the human potential groups were and are primarily therapeutic in orientation, it is part of the same cultural heritage. This ideological compatibility is obvious when humanists speak of the need for self-actualization, the need for humans to "experience their full potentialities," "to realize their own creative talents and desires," "to fulfill [their] unique capabilities," or when they speak of the "ultimate goal" of humanity as "the fulfillment of the potential growth in each human personality."[29] Humanism and the human potential movement thus share a common linguistic base. They also share a common ideological concern with the primacy of subjective experience. Given all of this, it is hardly surprising to learn of documentation that identifies the Association for Humanistic Psychology as "the professional and research wing of the [human potential] movement."[30] The movements are not only closely related, they are complementary.

Further, humanism, with its emphasis on "superior cognition" or "elite knowledge," displays many of the characteristics of gnostic sectarianism. The demographic base of the humanist movement in the higher echelons of scientific and professional training (unfrequented by the common man) as well as the penultimate value accorded to science and technology give credibility to the assertion that humanism is gnostic in its orientation. The sectarian quality of humanism is further suggested by its claims of universal validity, its sense of historical destiny, and its zeal to proselytize.[31]

In sum, humanism as described here clearly does fit certain sociological criteria of religion. Would it matter to this argument if the humanist activists rejected the term "religion" as self-descriptive? Not particularly. Neo-orthodox Christian theology has emphatically rejected the term too, as have a number of groups in the human potential movement (such as Transcendental Meditation). Yet this has not dissuaded most social scientists from regarding them theoretically and empirically as religions or quasi religions. It would be more difficult to use the term religion to describe humanism if humanists rejected it consistently, but the majority do not. Ethical Culture, for example, officially describes itself as a "religious fellowship" as does the Fellowship of Religious Humanists. Indeed, the preamble of the American Humanist Association states that the AHA is itself a "religious organization." Leaders in the popular movement—from Dewey to Lamont, from Kurtz to Beattie[32]—have repeatedly, or at key stages, identified humanism as a religion. (And might still be doing so were it not for recent tactical responses to recent fundamentalist attacks on secular humanism as a religion, which have had the ironic effect of strengthening the secularism in humanism.) Likewise, the *Humanist Manifesto I* is replete with expressions and inferences that imply humanism is a religion. Indeed, this document implies that humanism is the highest realization of man's *religious* aspirations.

Secular Humanism as Cultural Ethos

To concede that humanism comprises a religious or quasi-religious faith at this formal level is to concede very little. The obvious and more and more important question is, what does a "religion" for a marginal, though sometimes eminent, and largely (politically) powerless minority have to do with secular humanism in the larger culture? Few people would suggest that the followers, or even leaders, of humanism have much direct influence on many American institutions, particularly the public schools. Yet it would be equally facile to maintain that there is no relation between the formal ideology of the popular movement and developments in the larger culture—or that the relationship between movement humanism and the ideology of public education (if one exists) is purely coincidental. What, then, is the nature of that relationship?

To the extent that secular humanism exists in the larger culture, it does not as a formal ideological system (in the sense that it is formalized in the humanist movement), nor as a religion. As promulgated in the media or as taught in the public schools, humanism lacks the self-consciousness and articulation of a formal ideology. In any case, at this level it is clearly not a religion. Nevertheless, it is possible to speak of humanism as a latent moral ideology, a "folk" ideology or even a tacit faith. It is in this latent sense that the American social theorist, Talcott Parsons, spoke of secular humanism as America's fourth faith.[33] Likewise it is in this sense that constitutional scholar (and the father of separationist doctrine), Leo Pfeffer, described humanism earlier as "a religion along with the three major theistic faiths" (a position on which he has since changed his mind because of fundamentalist opposition).

But from what does this latent moral ideology derive? At one level, it derives from the intellectual traditions of the Enlightenment—an ideological revolution that led to the debunking of medieval and reformational cosmologies and the undermining of feudal forms of political authority and theistic forms of moral authority. Enshrined in their place were the commitments to scientific rationality and utopian visions of human progress and perfectibility—commitments that were embedded within the assumptions of philosophical naturalism.

But the Enlightenment—which was always less secular in America than in Europe—was not just a solitary event generated by French, English, and German intellectuals in the eighteenth century. These intellectual traditions have been carried down to succeeding generations even to the present. These traditions, then, have been institutionalized within certain sectors of post-Enlightenment society. The main "carriers" have been the intellectual classes, broadly understood—those who derive their livelihood from the knowledge sector—whether they be professors, journalists, media elites, lawyers, or educators. This sector of the population is distinguished by its access to higher education and thus to the institutions of intellectual rationality. Its members are also distinguished, as public opinion surveys indicate, by a general indifference toward traditional theistic beliefs and practices, if not by an outright secularity and a social and political liberalism (at least compared with the general population).[34] Peter Berger has called the ideology of the knowledge classes "secular humanism";[35] Alvin Gouldner has called it "the culture of critical discourse."[36] The terms essentially describe the same reality.

This point is vital because it is here also that one can locate the popular humanist movement sociologically. Its advocates may occupy only a tiny fraction of the intellectual classes, but their ideology represents a crystallization of the more diffuse ideological themes.

At still another level, the latent moral ideology of humanism derives from broader developments within modern life. The literature that evaluates change in American culture is voluminous and impossible to review here. Even so, at least two themes recur. The first concerns the increasing "rationalization" of the major institutional bureaucracies of contemporary society. It basically entails the impulse toward what Max Weber and his students have called "bureaucratization and disenchantment," what Jacques Ellul called "technological domination," what

Herbert Marcuse called rational "one-dimensionality," and what Robert Bellah has called "utilitarian individualism."

The second theme concerns the changing nature of life in the private sphere, the sphere of personal and family life, of personal relationships, and so on. These developments have been variously discussed as a tendency toward what Christopher Lasch, Richard Sennett, and others have called "narcissism," what Daniel Bell called "hedonism" or "antinomianism," what Arnold Gehlen called "subjectivism," what Phillip Rieff called the "therapeutic mentality," and what Bellah and his associate have called "expressive individualism." As numerous studies have made clear, these tendencies are particularly prominent within the highly educated upper-middle classes.

If social science has described these cultural tendencies with any accuracy, even in their general contours, then they can be seen as fitting comfortably with the formal ideology of movement humanism. That is, the latent moral ideology and the formal tenets of the sectarian movement share a common ideological structure. What this means, in turn, is that the structure of contemporary culture provides a "plausibility structure," or a reinforcing cultural context, within which humanistic ideology, both formal and "folk," becomes credible if not "common-sensical" to an increasing number of people.

Public Education and the Dominant Ideology

The claim that secular humanism is a pervasive ideology in American public life that has sometimes received the unofficial support of the state was tested in 1986 in *Smith* v. *Board of School Commissioners*, a case that pitted a coalition of evangelical Protestants, conservative Catholics, and other "theists"[37] against the Mobile, Alabama, Board of Education backed by, among others, the American Civil Liberties Union, and the People for the American Way.[38] The plaintiffs argued that many of the textbooks used in the county's public schools actually promoted the "religion of secular humanism" in violation of the no establishment provision of the First Amendment. These claims were widely discredited in the media and by activists, but viewed in light of a broader social scientific perspective rather than that of partisan politics, their credibility is harder to ignore.

First, public education is simply one of the massive public bureaucracies of modern society and, as such, has been subject to the same kind of "disenchantment" as other public bureaucracies. Second, evidence seems to indicate that there is a certain affinity between the ideological content of public education and the interests of certain cultural elites and the state. The argument can be framed this way.

Ever since its inception, the public school system has represented a government monopoly over mass education and therefore represents education from a particular perspective. Though that perspective may have changed over the course of 150 years, this point is as true today as it was in the early nineteenth century. A comparison may be instructive. In private schools, the curriculum tends to reflect the interests of the fee-paying clientele. These institutions depend directly on the capital resources of that clientele, and if the latter is dissatisfied and withdraw their children, the institutions would decline and collapse.

Public schools, on the other hand, are not so directly dependent on, and beholden to, their local constituencies—because these local constituencies are not the main source of their funds. Public education, then, is more likely to reflect the interests of the secular bureaucracy of the modern state from which it derives and on which it depends. It is also more likely to reflect the vested interests and cultural orientation of a larger category of cultural elites—not only those who design educational curricula but other arbiters of social taste and opinion (such as journalists, lawyers, professors, and so on).

Understood from this perspective, it is not surprising to find widespread evidence of the omission of almost all references to theistic religion in the description of American life and culture or of the American past in textbooks.[39] Such omissions not only distort the historical record, they contradict both the cultural background from which most American students come as well as the best recent scholarship in the universities to which many of them will go. In addition, they prejudice the educational process against theistic religion. The evidence also suggests that public school curricula reflect an emphasis on the individual as the measure of all things and on personal autonomy, feelings, personal needs, and subjectively derived values—all of which are independent of the transcendent standard implied in traditional theism.[40] To the extent that this is true, public education arguably shares a common ethical orientation with modern humanism, particularly to the degree that these perspectives are advanced without respect for cultural traditions that might dissent.

Interestingly, some of the more militant and secularist protagonists of humanism recognize and revel in these realities. Charles Francis Potter, one of the signers of the *Humanist Manifesto I* wrote: "Education is thus a most powerful ally of Humanism, and every American public school is a school of Humanism. What can the theistic Sunday schools, meeting for an hour once a week, and teaching only a fraction of the children, do to stem the tide of a five-day program of humanistic teaching?"[41]

Likewise, Paul Blanshard wrote in an essay in *The Humanist:* "I think the most important factor moving us toward a secular society has been the educational factor. Our schools may not teach Johnny to read properly, but the fact that Johnny is in school until he is sixteen tends toward the elimination of religious superstition."[42] Finally, though admittedly less eminent and less representative, John Dunphy argued in a much-cited letter: "I am convinced that the battle for humankind's future must be waged and won in the public school classrooms by teachers who correctly perceive their role as the proselytizers of a new faith: a religion of humanity. . . . These teachers must embody the same selfless dedication as the most rabid fundamentalist preachers, for they will be ministers of another sort, utilizing a classroom instead of a pulpit to convey humanist values."[43]

In many respects, the logic of all this evidence is unsurprising. It falls in line with many of the basic canons of sociological theory and cultural analysis: namely, no knowledge is value neutral; no knowledge is free of presuppositions. All knowledge is rooted in the social structure in particular ways and reflects (even if indirectly) the particular interests of different sectors of the population. Unquestionably, this also holds true for the "knowledge" passed on to children in public schools.

The initial judgement in *Smith* v. *Board of School Commissioners* decided in favor of the plaintiffs' arguments, and though it was eventually overturned, the case raised critical issues about public education and its tendency to reflect the dominant moral ideology of public life. As Professor Robert Coles of Harvard University, who was the lead witness for the defense put it, "I don't know if there is a religion called 'secular humanism,' but there is definitely a 'secular religion' in education today."[44] *Washington Post* columnist, Colman McCarthy, also found himself unable to support the detractors of the plaintiffs. Writing in the *Washington Post* McCarthy wrote: "There's one hitch in all this: the actual 111-page decision of Judge Hand. It is not another spray of right-wing dye meant to color the debate with the biases of backwoods Bible-toters. A careful reading of the decision, as against a skimming of news accounts of it, reveals that Mobile families had a fair grievance: That what was taught in classrooms about religion was impeding the teachings of mothers and fathers at home about religion. What's wrong with that complaint?"[45]

In Search of Public Justice

In the end, the reality of "secular humanism" and its status and influence in contemporary life is much more complicated than most leading activists would have. Secular humanism in American public life is neither an all-embracing and self-aggrandizing religion conspiring to control American institutions, nor is it a fiction manufactured by the religious right as a scapegoat for all the problems they see. Where secular humanism can be described accurately as a sectarian religion, it has almost no impact on American institutions. Yet where it does have an impact (as the latent moral ideology of the intellectual classes, of the media of mass communications and of public education, and the like) it does so as a relatively diffuse moral ethos rather than as a religion.

To describe it as a relatively diffuse moral ethos is not to say it is indistinct and culturally impotent. Quite the opposite. Indeed, the evidence points to the fact that it occupies much the same place in American public culture as nondenominational Protestantism in the nineteenth century. Because of its specific role in the contemporary public school curricula, it actually enjoys the status of a quasi establishment. There is deep irony in this fact. Evangelicals and other theists who protest against the quasi establishment of secular humanism have taken roughly the same position as the Catholic hierarchy in the mid-nineteenth century in their protest against the quasi establishment of

Protestantism. For their part, ideological progressives, such as the American Civil Liberties Union and the People for the American Way, occupy much the same position assumed by their evangelical Protestant counterparts a century before. They share a strong interest in maintaining both the status quo and their own dominant position in it.

What does all of this mean for the conduct of law on this issue? To be legally consistent the courts will either have to articulate a constitutional double standard or apply the functional definition of religion to the no establishment clause just as they have to the free exercise. The latter would mean that secularistic faiths and ideologies would be rigorously prohibited from receiving even indirect support from the state, which—needless to say—would have enormous implications for public education. The potential consequences of this outcome are alarming to many progressive constitutional scholars, not least (the sociologist of knowledge might infer) because it would operate counter to their interests. They therefore vigorously reject consistency in favor of what they themselves call a "double standard"–a functional definition of religion for free exercise purposes and a substantive definition for no establishment purposes. Without such a double standard, Laurence Tribe has reasoned, every humane government program could be "deemed constitutionally suspect."[46]

Yet, if the courts adopt such a double standard, what possibly could provide a set of fair ground rules for value-grounded debate? Debating whether a cultural system or faith is religious (strictly speaking) becomes an exercise in arid legalism that is almost beside the point. If part of the moral purpose of the religious liberty clauses was to establish a mechanism of public justice whereby no one faith or ideology would have a government-based advantage over another, how could there be fairness between traditional theists and nontheists or progressive theists if the courts do not acknowledge the incalculable advantages afforded to the latter through such a constitutional double standard?

In the end, the religion clauses of the First Amendment concern both rights and responsibilities—the right to live according to the convictions of conscience without state interference and coercion, and the responsibility to respect that right for others, including the repudiation of all direct and indirect patronage of the state, whether for others or oneself. Today the religion clauses must contend with social and cultural conditions that are fundamentally different from those that confronted the framers. But the ideal of public justice that those clauses aspire to establish has not changed. Reconciling that ideal with novel social conditions, and in particular the place of secular beliefs in the current expansion of pluralism, is the challenge that we, the heirs and benefactors of the founders' moral project, must now face.

Freedom of Conscience or Freedom of Choice?

MICHAEL J. SANDEL

ONE OF THE PREVAILING hypotheses of the contemporary public debate is that the reigning public philosophy is inadequate or impoverished in ways that a larger public role for religion might help to cure. In order to assess this claim, it may be helpful to examine the political theory of contemporary liberalism and to describe its stance toward religious practice and belief. In one respect, the liberal tradition seeks to secure for religion the most favorable conditions; given its emphasis on toleration and respect for conscience, liberal political theory promises the fullest religious liberty for each consistent with a similar liberty for all. In another respect, however, liberalism limits the reach of religion; its insistence that government be neutral among competing moral and theological visions, that political authority be justified without reference to religious sanction, would seem to confine religion to private life and to resist a public role.

The question whether government can be neutral among competing moral and religious conceptions is the subject of much debate within recent political philosophy. The goal here is threefold: the first is to summarize this debate, and to argue, briefly, that government cannot be neutral in this sense. The second is to show that, notwithstanding its inadequacy as theory, this version of liberalism is the one that has come to inform the constitutional law of religious liberty. I try finally to show how problems in the theory find expression in the law.

Liberalism and the Unencumbered Self

The version of liberalism with which I am concerned is prominent in contemporary moral, legal, and political philosophy. Its central idea is that government should be neutral on the question of the good life.[1] Since people disagree on the best way to live, public policy should be "independent of any particular conception of the good life, or of what gives value to life."[2]

This version of liberalism is defined by the claim that the right is prior to the good, and in two senses: first, individual rights cannot be sacrificed for the sake of the general good; and second, the principles of justice that specify these rights cannot be premised on any particular vision of the good life. What justifies the rights is not that they maximize the general welfare or otherwise promote the good, but rather that they comprise a fair framework within which individuals can choose their own values and ends, consistent with a similar liberty for others.

The claim for the priority of the right over the good derives much of its moral force from a certain conception of the person. Unlike utilitarianism, which assumes a self simply defined as the sum of its desires, the liberal ethic affirms the notion of a choosing self, independent of the desires and ends it may have at any moment. Thus Kant appealed to the idea of a moral subject given prior to experience, capable of an autonomous will. And contemporary liberals rely on the similar idea of a self given prior to its purposes and ends.

For purposes of politics and law, this conception of the person seems compelling for at least two reasons. First, the image of the self as free and independent, unencumbered by aims and attachments it does not choose for itself, offers a powerful liberating vision. Freed from the sanctions of custom and tradition and inherited status, unbound by moral ties antecedent to choice, the liberal self is installed as sovereign, cast as the author of the only obligations that constrain. More than the simple sum of circumstance, we become capable of the dignity that consists in being persons of our "own creating, making, choosing."[3] We are agents and not just instruments of the purposes we pursue. We are "self-originating sources of valid claims."[4]

A second appeal of the liberal self-image consists in the case it implies for equal respect. The idea that there is more to a person than the roles he plays or the customs she keeps or the faith he affirms suggests a basis for respect independent of life's contingencies. Liberal justice is blind to such differences between persons as race, religion, ethnicity, and gender, for in the liberal self-image, these features do not really define identity in the first place. They are not constituents but merely attributes of the self, the sort of things the state should look beyond.

These considerations help clarify the connection between the aspiration to neutrality and the unencumbered self. If we conceive ourselves as free and independent selves, unclaimed by moral ties antecedent to choice, we must be governed by a neutral framework, a framework of rights that refuses to choose among competing purposes and ends. If the self is prior to its ends, then the right must be prior to the good.

But how plausible is this self-conception? Can it make sense of our moral life, at least in those aspects relevant to politics and law? I shall first suggest some general reasons for thinking that it cannot, then turn to the specific case of religion.

One general difficulty with the liberal self-image is that it limits in advance the kind of community of which we are capable, and implausibly restricts the scope of moral and political obligation.[5] Understood as unencumbered selves, we are free to join in voluntary association with others, whether to advance our private ends, or to enjoy the communal sentiments that such associations often inspire. We might call this community in the cooperative sense.

What is denied to the unencumbered self is the possibility of membership in any community bound by moral ties antecedent to choice; he cannot belong to any community where the self itself could be at stake. Such a community would engage the identity as well as the interests of the participants, and so implicate its members in a citizenship more thoroughgoing than the unencumbered self can know. More than a cooperative arrangement, community in this second, stronger sense describes a mode of self-understanding, a shared way of life that partly defines the identity of the participants. We might call it community in the constitutive sense.

One way of distinguishing communities in the constitutive sense from those that are merely cooperative is by reference to the moral and political obligations the participants acknowledge. On the liberal view, obligations can only arise in one of two ways, as "natural duties" we owe to human beings as such, or as voluntary obligations we incur by consent. The natural duties are the duties we owe persons *qua* persons—to do justice, to avoid cruelty, and so on. All other obligations, the ones we owe to particular others, are founded in consent, and can only arise in virtue of agreements we make, be they tacit or explicit.[6]

Conceived as unencumbered selves, we must respect the dignity of all persons, but beyond this, we owe only what we agree to owe. Liberal justice requires that we respect people's rights (as defined by the neutral framework), not that we advance their good. Whether we must concern ourselves with other people's good depends on whether, and with whom, and on what terms, we have agreed to do so.

The liberal attempt to construe all obligation in terms of duties universally owed or obligations voluntarily incurred makes it difficult to account for a wide range of moral and political ties that we commonly recognize. It fails to capture those loyalties and responsibilities whose moral force consists partly in the fact that living by them is inseparable from understanding ourselves as the particular persons we are—as members of this family or city or nation or people, as bearers of that history, as citizens of this republic. Loyalties such as these can be more than values I happen to have, and to hold, at a certain distance. The moral responsibilities they entail may go beyond the obligations I voluntarily incur and the "natural duties" I owe to human beings as such. Those who share a common life informed by moral ties such as these may be said to comprise a community in the constitutive sense. The meaning of their membership cannot be redescribed without loss in wholly voluntarist or contractarian terms.

In the sections to follow, I explore this general objection to contemporary liberalism by considering the case of religion. I shall try to show that the version of liberalism I have summarized informs the current understanding of religious liberty in American constitutional law, and that difficulties in the theory show up in the practice. I shall try also to show that the reigning interpretation of religious liberty is not characteristic of the American constitutional tradition as such, but a recent development that departs from earlier understandings.

MICHAEL J. SANDEL

Religion and the Constitution:
The Search for Neutrality

After World War II, the U.S. Supreme Court assumed as its primary role the protection of individual rights against government infringement. Increasingly, it defined these rights according to the requirement that government be neutral on the question of the good life, and defended neutrality as essential to respecting persons as free and independent selves, unencumbered by moral ties antecedent to choice.

The principle of government neutrality found its first sustained application in cases involving religion. Time and again the Supreme Court has held that "in the relationship between man and religion, the State is firmly committed to a position of neutrality."[7] "Government in our democracy, state and nation, must be neutral in matters of religious theory, doctrine, and practice. . . . The First Amendment mandates governmental neutrality between religion and religion, and between religion and nonreligion."[8] Whether described as "a strict and lofty neutrality,"[9] a "wholesome neutrality,"[10] or a "benevolent neutrality,"[11] the principle "that the Government must pursue a course of complete neutrality toward religion"[12] is well established in American constitutional law.

In liberal political thought, religion offers the paradigmatic case for bracketing controversial conceptions of the good.[13] The Supreme Court has conveyed its insistence on bracketing religion by invoking Jefferson's metaphor of a "wall of separation between church and state."[14] While some complained that "a rule of law should not be drawn from a figure of speech,"[15] most see the wall as a symbol of resolve to keep religion from bursting the constitutional brackets that contain it. Since "the breach of neutrality that is today a trickling stream may all too soon become a raging torrent,"[16] the "wall between Church and State . . . must be kept high and impregnable."[17]

It is striking to recall that, for all its familiarity, the requirement that government be neutral on matters of religion is not a long-standing principle of constitutional law, but a recent arrival, a development of the last forty years. Not until 1947 did the Supreme Court hold that government must be neutral toward religion.[18] The American tradition of religious liberty goes back further of course. The Con-

78

stitution forbids religious tests for federal office,[19] and the first words of the First Amendment declare that "Congress shall make no law respecting an establishment of religion, or prohibiting the free exercise thereof." But the Bill of Rights did not apply to the states, and at the time of its adoption, six of the thirteen states maintained religious establishments.[20] Far from prohibiting these arrangements, the First Amendment was enacted in part to protect state religious establishments from federal interference.[21]

Within the states, the most eventful struggle for the separation of church and state occurred in Virginia, not least because Jefferson and Madison waged it. In 1776 the legislature disestablished the Anglican church, but left open the possibility of a "general assessment," or tax for the support of religion. Jefferson argued for complete separation of church and state, and in "A Bill for Establishing Religious Freedom" (1779), proposed that "no man shall be compelled to frequent or support any religious worship, place, or ministry whatsoever."[22]

After several years of inconclusive debate, Patrick Henry introduced a general assessment bill to support "teachers of the Christian Religion." Under Henry's proposal, each taxpayer could designate which Christian church would receive his tax. Henry defended his plan on the nonsectarian grounds that the diffusion of Christian knowledge would help "correct the morals of men, restrain their vices, and preserve the peace of society." Madison led the opposition, and wrote a pamphlet, "Memorial and Remonstrance against Religious Assessments" (1785), that helped turn opinion against the bill. After defeating the general assessment, Madison won passage of Jefferson's bill guaranteeing separation of church and state.[23]

Some states did not disestablish religion until well into the nineteenth century. Connecticut continued tax support for religion until 1818, Massachusetts until 1833. New Jersey restricted full civil rights to Protestants until 1844, and Maryland required belief in God as a condition of public office until the U.S. Supreme Court struck it down in 1961.[24] Even in states without establishments, some nineteenth-century courts held Christianity to be part of the common law. In a New York case in 1811, Chancellor James Kent upheld a conviction for blasphemy on the ground that "we are a Christian people, and the morality of the country is deeply ingrafted upon Christianity."[25]

79

In 1845 the U.S. Supreme Court reiterated with respect to the religious liberty clauses its view that the Bill of Rights did not constrain the states. "The Constitution makes no provision for protecting the citizens of the respective states in their religious liberties; this is left to the state constitutions and laws."[26] As far as the U.S. Constitution was concerned, the states were free to establish a church or "to recreate the Inquisition," at least until the adoption of the Fourteenth Amendment.[27]

Even after the adoption of the Fourteenth Amendment, attempts to assert government neutrality toward religion confronted difficulty. In 1876 President Ulysses Grant spoke out against public support for sectarian schools, and fellow Republican James G. Blaine introduced in Congress a constitutional amendment to that end: "No State shall make any law respecting an establishment of religion or prohibiting the free exercise thereof; and no money raised by taxation in any state for the support of public schools . . . shall ever be under the control of any religious sect or denomination." The amendment passed the House but was defeated in the Senate, partly because of Catholic opposition, partly because of a belief that existing constitutional protections were adequate.[28]

Two years later, the U.S. Supreme Court upheld a federal law banning polygamy, a practice the Mormons regarded as a religious duty. In *Reynolds* v. *United States* (1878), a Mormon convicted under the statute complained it denied him the free exercise of religion guaranteed in the First Amendment. After citing Madison's "Memorial and Remonstrance" and Jefferson's "wall of separation," the Court nonetheless upheld the conviction, arguing that the First Amendment protected religious belief but not practice. "Polygamy has always been odious" among Western nations, the Court declared, adding that polygamy was less conducive than monogamy to democratic government.[29]

Not until the 1940s did the Court apply the First Amendment's religious liberty clauses to the states and declare the separation of church and state a principle of constitutional law. In *Cantwell* v. *Connecticut* (1940), the Court held that the Fourteenth Amendment incorporated both the establishment and free exercise clauses of the Bill of Rights, and "rendered the legislatures of the states as incompetent as Congress to enact such laws."[30] In *Everson* v. *Board of Education of*

Ewing Township (1947), the Court gave the establishment clause a broad interpretation and emphasized, for the first time, Jefferson's "wall of separation between church and state."[31]

Writing for the Court, Justice Black gave forceful expression to the principle of government neutrality. "Neither a state nor the Federal Government can set up a church. Neither can pass laws which aid one religion, aid all religions, or prefer one religion over another. . . . No tax in any amount, large or small, can be levied to support any religious activities or institutions." The First Amendment "requires the state to be a neutral in its relations with groups of religious believers and non-believers."[32]

Since *Everson*, religion has generated much constitutional controversy, but the principle that government must be neutral toward religion has rarely been questioned.[33] For the most part, the justices have cast their disagreements as arguments about the proper application of neutrality, not about the principle itself. In fact, Black's landmark opinion in *Everson* came in the course of upholding a state subsidy for bus transportation of parochial school students. The dissenters applauded the Court's insistence on "complete and uncompromising separation" but found it "utterly discordant" with the result in the case.[34]

In 1963, the Court ruled that Bible reading in the public schools was a religious exercise at odds with the requirement "that the Government maintain strict neutrality, neither aiding nor opposing religion."[35] Justice Stewart dissented, but in the name of neutrality. Permission of religious exercises is necessary, he argued, "if the schools are truly to be neutral in the matter of religion. And a refusal to permit religious exercises thus is seen, not as the realization of state neutrality, but rather as the establishment of a religion of secularism, or at the least, as government support of the beliefs of those who think that religious exercises should be conducted only in private."[36]

In 1968 the Court struck down an Arkansas law that banned the teaching of evolution. "Government must be neutral in matters of religious theory, doctrine, and practice," wrote Justice Fortas. "It may not be hostile to any religion." In a concurring opinion, Justice Black agreed with the result but doubted that the principle of neutrality supported it. If Darwinism contradicts some people's religious convictions, then it is hardly neutral to teach it in the public schools. "If the

81

theory is considered anti-religious, how can the State be bound by the Federal Constitution to permit its teachers to advocate such an 'anti-religious' doctrine to school children?"[37]

Black pointed out that the Court might simply take the view that fundamentalists who regard evolution as antireligious are wrong. But that would be taking sides in the controversy the Court purports to bracket. "Unless this Court is prepared simply to write off as pure nonsense the views of those who consider evolution an anti-religious doctrine," Black argued, the issue is more difficult than the Court acknowledges. A better way to bracket, he suggested, might be to remove the controversial subject from the schools altogether, as Arkansas arguably did. So long as the biblical account of creation is not taught instead, "does not the removal of the subject of evolution leave the State in a neutral position toward these supposedly competing religious and anti-religious doctrines?"[38]

The contest for the mantle of neutrality continued in 1985, when the Court struck down a moment-of-silence statute permitting voluntary prayer in Alabama schools. The Court held that since the purpose of the law was to restore prayer to the schools, it violated "the established principle that the Government must pursue a course of complete neutrality toward religion." Chief Justice Burger dissented, arguing that the prohibition "manifests not neutrality but hostility toward religion."[39]

Even in cases where the Supreme Court has upheld government involvement in arguably religious practices, it has taken pains to maintain that the religious aspect is only incidental, that the involvement does not endorse or advance or prefer religion. In *McGowan* v. *Maryland* (1961), the Court upheld Sunday Closing laws on the grounds that they no longer retain their religious character. Notwithstanding their religious origins, wrote Chief Justice Warren, laws prohibiting business and commercial activity on Sundays now serve the secular purpose of "providing a Sunday atmosphere of recreation, cheerfulness, repose and enjoyment. . . . The air of the day is one of relaxation rather than obe of religion."[40]

In 1984 the Burger Court upheld on similar grounds a city-sponsored Christmas display including a creche, or Nativity scene. The purpose of the display is to celebrate the holiday and to depict its origins, the Court held. "These are legitimate secular purposes." Any benefit it brings to religion "is indirect, remote and incidental." Display of the creche is no more an advancement or endorsement of religion than the exhibition of religious paintings in governmentally supported museums.[41]

In both cases, dissenters criticized the Court for failing to take seriously the religious character of the practices they upheld. "No matter what is said, the parentage of the Sunday Closing laws is the Fourth Commandment," wrote Justice Douglas. "They serve and satisfy the religious predispositions of our Christian communities."[42] Dissenting in the creche case, Justice Blackmun complained that the majority had done "an injustice to the creche and the message it manifests." In the hands of the Court, "The creche has been relegated to the role of a neutral harbinger of the holiday season, useful for commercial purposes, but devoid of any inherent meaning and incapable of enhancing the religious tenor of a display of which it is an integral part. . . . Surely, this is a misuse of a sacred symbol."[43]

Religion and the Constitution: Justifying Neutrality

In order to assess the Court's conflicting applications of neutrality, it is necessary to consider the reasons for neutrality. What counts as neutrality partly depends on what justifies neutrality, and the Court has offered two different sorts of justification for insisting that government be neutral toward religion.

The first has to do with protecting the interests of religion on the one hand, and of the state on the other. "The First Amendment rests on the premise that both religion and government can best work to achieve their lofty aims if each is left free from the other within its respective sphere."[44] "We have staked the very existence of our country on the fact that complete separation between the state and religion is best for the state and best for religion."[45] "In the long view the independence of both church and state in their respective spheres will be better served by close adherence to the neutrality principle."[46]

The religious interest served by separation lies in avoiding the corruption that comes with dependence on civil authority. A century and a half before Jefferson stated the secular case for a "wall of separation" between church and state, Roger Williams gave the metaphor a theological meaning. "When they have opened a gap in the hedge or wall of separation between the garden of the church and the wilderness of the world," he wrote, "God hath ever broke down the wall itself, removed the candlestick, and made His garden a wilderness, as at this day."[47]

The Court has invoked the theological argument for separation only occasionally, and usually in combination with other arguments. In striking down school prayer, for example, Justice Black argued that the establishment clause "rested on the belief that a union of government and religion tends to destroy government and to degrade religion." The history of established religion "showed that many people lost their respect for any religion that had relied upon the support of government to spread its faith." The founders sought by the establishment clause to avoid the "unhallowed perversion" of religion by a civil magistrate.[48] And Justice Brennan emphasized that separation is not only for the sake of the nonbeliever but also for "the devout believer who fears the secularization of a creed which becomes too deeply involved with and dependent upon the government."[49]

The political interest served by separation is in avoiding the civil strife that has historically attended church-state entanglements. Providing public funds for religion brings "the struggle of sect against sect. . . . It is only by observing the prohibition rigidly that the state can maintain its neutrality and avoid partisanship in the dissensions inevitable when sect opposes sect over demands for public moneys."[50] Opposing public school involvement in a "released time" program for religious instruction, Justice Frankfurter wrote that "the public school must be kept scrupulously free from entanglement in the strife of sects."[51] In a similar case, Justice Black vividly recalled the danger of sectarian strife that separation was meant to prevent. "Colonial history had already shown that, here as elsewhere zealous sectarians entrusted with governmental power to further their causes would sometimes torture, maim and kill those they branded heretics, atheists or agnostics."[52]

Alongside the argument that neutrality is best for religion and best for the state is a different sort of argument, an argument in the name of individual freedom. On this justification, the state must be neutral not only to avoid compromising religion and provoking sectarian strife, but also to avoid the danger of coercion. This argument goes back to the eighteenth-century concern for freedom of conscience, and in its modern form emphasizes respect for persons' freedom to choose their religious convictions for themselves. It thus connects the case for neutrality with the liberal conception of the person.

In its modern, or voluntarist version, this argument for religious liberty first appears in *Cantwell*, the case that announced the incorporation of the religious liberty clauses. "Freedom of conscience and freedom to adhere to such religious organization or form of worship *as the individual may choose* cannot be restricted by law." The First Amendment "safeguards the free exercise of the chosen form of religion."[53]

In banning Bible reading in the public schools, the Court found justification for neutrality in "the right of every person to freely choose his own course" with reference to religion, "free of any compulsion from the state." Justice Stewart dissented from the result, but endorsed the view that neutrality is required for the sake of respect for individual choice, "a refusal on the part of the state to weight the scales of private choice."[54]

Contemporary commentators have identified the voluntarist argument for neutrality as the primary justification for the separation of church and state. "The fundamental principle underlying both Religion clauses is the protection of individual choice in matters of religion—whether pro or con."[55] "Since freedom of religious choice, not neutrality per se, is the fundamental establishment value, the neutrality tool is useful only insofar as it promotes that choice."[56] "The moral basis of the antiestablishment clause is . . . equal respect," not for religious beliefs themselves but "for the processes of forming and changing such conceptions."[57] In short, the religious liberty clauses secure "the core ideal of religious autonomy."[58]

Perhaps the clearest statement of the voluntarist conception of religious liberty is the one that appears in Justice Stevens's opinion for the Court in a 1985 case striking down Alabama's moment of silence for voluntary prayer in public schools. "The individual's freedom to choose his own creed is the counterpart of his right to refrain from accepting the creed established by the majority," Stevens wrote. "The

Court has unambiguously concluded that the individual freedom of conscience protected by the First Amendment embraces the right to select any religious faith or none at all. This conclusion derives support not only from the interest in respecting the individual's freedom of conscience, but also from the conviction that *religious beliefs worthy of respect are the product of free and voluntary choice* by the faithful." [59]

As Stevens's opinion illustrates, the voluntarist justification of neutrality presupposes the liberal conception of the person. It holds that government should be neutral toward religion in order to respect persons as free and independent selves, capable of choosing their religious convictions for themselves. The respect this neutrality commands is not, strictly speaking, respect for religion, but respect for the self whose religion it is, or respect for the dignity that consists in the capacity to choose one's religion freely. Religious beliefs are "worthy of respect," not in virtue of what they are beliefs in, but rather in virtue of being "the product of free and voluntary choice," in virtue of being beliefs of a self unencumbered by convictions antecedent to choice.

By invoking the voluntarist conception of neutrality, the Court gives constitutional expression to the version of liberalism that conceives the right as prior to the good and the self as prior to its ends, at least where religion is concerned. We are now in a position to see how the promise of the theory, but also its problems, make themselves felt in the practice the theory informs. We turn first to the promise.

The voluntarist case for neutrality, insisting as it does on respect for persons, seems to secure for religious liberty a firm foundation. Unlike the theological case for separation of church and state, it does not depend on any particular religious doctrine. And unlike the political case for separation, it does not leave religious liberty hostage to uncertain calculations about how best to avoid civil strife. Under present conditions, such calculations may or may not support the separation of church and state. As Justice Powell has observed, the risk "of deep political division along religious lines" is by now "remote." [60] We do not live on the brink of the wars of religion that gave toleration its first occasion.

Even granting the importance of avoiding sectarian strife, a strict separation of church and state may at times provoke more strife than it prevents. The school prayer decisions of the early sixties, for example, set off a storm of political controversy that twenty-five years have not stilled.[61] A court concerned above all to avoid social discord might reasonably have decided those cases the other way.

The voluntarist case for neutrality, by contrast, does not tie religious liberty to such contingencies. In affirming a notion of respect for persons, it recalls the ideal of freedom of conscience. By emphasizing the individual's right to choose his beliefs, it points beyond religion to "the broader perspective" of autonomy rights in general, including "the rights of privacy and personhood."[62] It thus casts religious liberty as a particular case of the liberal claim for the priority of the right over the good and the self-image that attends it. Respecting persons as selves defined prior to the religious convictions they affirm becomes a particular case of the general principle of respect for selves defined prior to their aims and attachments.

But as we have seen, the image of the unencumbered self, despite its appeal, is inadequate to the liberty it promises. In the case of religion, the liberal conception of the person ill equips the Court to secure religious liberty for those who regard themselves as claimed by religious commitments they have not chosen. Not all religious beliefs can be redescribed without loss as "the product of free and voluntary choice by the faithful."[63]

Freedom of Conscience versus Freedom of Choice

This can be seen by contrasting the voluntarist account of religious liberty with freedom of conscience as traditionally conceived. For Madison and Jefferson, freedom of conscience meant the freedom to exercise religious liberty—to worship or not, to support a church or not, to profess belief or disbelief—without suffering civil penalties or incapacities. It had nothing to do with a right to choose one's beliefs. Madison's "Memorial and Remonstrance" consists of fifteen arguments for the separation of church and state and not one makes any mention of "autonomy" or "choice."[64] The only choice referred to in Jefferson's Bill for Establishing Religious Freedom "is predicated of God, not man."[65]

Madison and Jefferson understood religious liberty as the right to exercise religious duties according to the dictates of conscience, not the right to choose religious beliefs. In fact, their argument for religious liberty relies heavily on the assumption that beliefs are not a matter of choice. The first sentence of Jefferson's bill states this assumption clearly: "The opinions and beliefs of men depend not on their own will, but follow involuntarily the evidence proposed to their own minds."[66] Since I can only believe what I am persuaded is true, belief is not the sort of thing that coercion can compel. Coercion can produce hypocrisy but not conviction. In this assumption Jefferson echoed the view of John Locke, who wrote in *A Letter Concerning Toleration* (1685), "It is absurd that things should be enjoined by laws which are not in men's power to perform. And to believe this or that to be true, does not depend upon our will."[67]

It is precisely because belief is not governed by the will that freedom of conscience is unalienable. Even if he would, a person could not give it up. This was Madison's argument in "Memorial and Remonstrance." "The Religion then of every man must be left to the conviction and conscience of every man; and it is the right of every man to exercise it as these may dictate. This right is in its nature an unalienable right. It is unalienable, because the opinions of men, depending only on the evidence contemplated by their own minds cannot follow the dictates of other men: it is unalienable also, because what is here a right towards men, is a duty towards the Creator."[68]

Oddly enough, Justice Stevens cites this passage from Madison in support of the voluntarist view. But freedom of conscience and freedom of choice are not the same; where conscience dictates, choice decides. Where freedom of conscience is at stake, the relevant right is to exercise a duty, not make a choice. This was the issue for Madison and Jefferson. Religious liberty addressed the problem of encumbered selves, claimed by duties they cannot renounce, even in the face of civil obligations that may conflict.

In contemporary liberalism, by contrast, religious liberty serves the broader mission of protecting individual autonomy. On this view, government should be neutral toward religion for the same reason it should be neutral toward competing conceptions of the good life generally—to respect people's capacity to choose their own values and ends. But despite its liberating promise, or perhaps because of it, this broader mission depreciates the claims of those for whom religion is not an expression of autonomy but a matter of conviction unrelated to a choice. Protecting religion as a "life-style," as one among the values that an independent self may have, may miss the role that religion plays in the lives of those for whom the observance of religious duties is a constitutive end, essential to their good and indispensable to their identity. Treating persons as "self-originating sources of valid claims"[69] may thus fail to respect persons bound by duties derived from sources other than themselves.

The case of *Thorton* v. *Caldor, Inc.* (1985) shows how voluntarist assumptions can crowd out religious liberty for encumbered selves. By an 8-1 decision, the Supreme Court struck down a Connecticut statute guaranteeing Sabbath observers a right not to work on their Sabbath.[70] Although the law gave all workers the right to one day off each week, it gave to Sabbath observers alone the right to designate their day. In this lack of neutrality the Court found constitutional infirmity.

Chief Justice Burger, writing for the Court, noted that Sabbath observers would typically take a weekend day, "widely prized as a day off." But "other employees who have strong and legitimate, but non-religious reasons for wanting a weekend day off have no rights under the statute." They "must take a back seat to the Sabbath observers." Justice O'Connor echoed this worry in a concurring opinion. "All employees, regardless of their religious orientation, would value the benefit which the statute bestows on Sabbath observers—the right to select the day of the week in which to refrain from labor."[71]

But this objection confuses the right to exercise a duty with the right to make a choice. Sabbath observers, by definition, do not select the day of the week they rest; they rest on the day their religion requires. The benefit the statute confers is not the right to choose a day of rest, but the right to exercise the duty of Sabbath observance on the only day it can be exercised.

Considered together with earlier decisions upholding Sunday Closing laws, *Thorton* v. *Caldor* yields a curious constitutional conclusion: a state may require everyone to rest on Sunday, the day of the Christian Sabbath, so long as the aim is not to accommodate the observance of the Sabbath. But it may not give Sabbath observers the right to rest on the day of the week their religion requires. Perverse though this result may seem from the standpoint of promoting religious pluralism, it aptly reflects the constitutional consequences of seeing ourselves as unencumbered selves.

The Court has on occasion accorded greater respect to the claims of encumbered selves. When a Seventh-day Adventist was fired from her job for refusing to work on Saturday, her Sabbath, she was denied unemployment compensation under a rule requiring applicants to accept available work. The Supreme Court decided in her favor, holding that the state could not force a worker to choose between her religious convictions and means of support. According to the Court, requiring the state to take account of Sabbath observance in the administration of its unemployment program did not prefer religion in violation of neutrality. Rather, it enforced "the governmental obligation of neutrality in the face of religious differences." In this case at least, the Constitution was not blind to religion but alive to its imperatives.[72]

In cases involving conscientious objection to military service, the Court has interpreted federal law broadly and refused to restrict exemptions to those with theistic beliefs alone. The relevant test is "whether a given belief that is sincere and meaningful occupies a place in the life of its possessor parallel to that filled by the orthodox belief in God."[73] What matters is not "conventional piety" but an imperative of conscience rising above the level of a policy preference.[74] The point of the exemption, according to the Court, is to prevent persons bound by moral duties they cannot renounce from having either to violate those duties or violate the law. This aim is consistent with Madison and Jefferson's concern for the predicament of persons claimed by dictates of conscience they are not at liberty to choose. As the Court wrote, "the painful dilemma of the sincere conscientious objector arises precisely because he feels himself bound in conscience not to compromise his beliefs or affiliations."[75]

In *Wisconsin* v. *Yoder* (1972), the Court upheld the right of the Old Order Amish not to send their children to school beyond the eighth grade, despite a state law requiring school attendance until age sixteen. Higher education would expose Amish children to worldly and competitive values contrary to the insular, agrarian way of life that sustains Amish community and religious practice. The Court emphasized that the Amish claim was "not merely a matter of personal preference, but one of deep religious conviction" that pervades their way of life.

Though "neutral on its face," Wisconsin's school attendance law unduly burdened the free exercise of religion, and so offended "the constitutional requirement for governmental neutrality."[76]

Writing in dissent, Justice Douglas asserted the voluntarist vision, arguing that the Amish children should be free to choose for themselves whether to continue in school or adopt the ways of their parents. "If a parent keeps his child out of school beyond the grade school, then the child will be forever barred from entry into the new and amazing world of diversity that we have today. The child may decide that that is the preferred course, or he may rebel." It is the child, not the parents who should be heard if the Court is to respect "the right of students to be masters of their own destiny."[77]

The Court's occasional hospitality to the claims of encumbered selves did not extend to Captain Simcha Goldman, an Orthodox Jew whom the Air Force prohibited from wearing a yarmulke while on duty in the health clinic where he served. Justice Rehnquist, writing for the Court, held for the Air Force on grounds of judicial deference to the "professional judgment of military authorities" on the importance of uniform dress.[78] Of the precedents he cited in support of deference to the military, all involved interests other than religious duties or conscientious imperatives. "The essence of military service 'is the subordination of the desires and interests of the individual to the needs of the service.'" Standardized uniforms encourage "the subordination of personal preferences and identities in favor of the overall mission." Having compared the wearing of a yarmulke to "desires," "interests," and "personal preferences" unrelated to religion, Rehnquist did not require the Air Force to show that an exception for yarmulkes would impair its disciplinary objectives. Nor did he even acknowledge that a religious duty was at stake, allowing only that, given the dress code, "military life may be more objectionable for petitioner."[79]

The Court's tendency to assimilate religious liberty to liberty in general reflects the aspiration to neutrality; people should be free to pursue their own interests and ends, whatever they are, consistent with a similar liberty for others. But this generalizing tendency does not always serve religious liberty well. It confuses the pursuit of preferences with the exercise of duties and so forgets the special concern of religious liberty with the claims of conscientiously encumbered selves.

This confusion has led the Court to restrict religious practices it should permit, such as yarmulkes in the military, and also to permit practices it should probably restrict, such as Nativity scenes in the public square. In different ways, both decisions fail to take religion seriously. Permitting Pawtucket's creche might seem to be a ruling sympathetic to religion. But as Justice Blackmun rightly protested, the Court's permission came at the price of denying the sacred meaning of the symbol it protected.

What has preceded attempts to show how the version of liberalism implicit in contemporary constitutional law depreciates the claims of religion and fails to respect persons bound by duties they have not chosen. To this extent, this version of liberalism fails to secure the toleration it promises. But beyond the issue of toleration is the further question whether the liberal self-image is adequate to the demands of self-government. Is the unencumbered self too thin to sustain the obligations of citizenship? If so, is religion among the forms of identity likely to generate a fuller citizenship and a more vital public life? Or does it depend on the religion; might some religious convictions erode rather than enhance the civic virtues required of citizens in a pluralistic society? These are questions this chapter can only suggest. Perhaps an attempt to address them would itself enrich the discourse of American public life.

SIX

Religion in a Free Society

CHARLES TAYLOR

WHAT IS THE PLACE of religion in a free, self-governing society? For some of the strands of thought that make up modern liberalism, the answer to this question is "none," or perhaps more accurately, religion is firmly relegated to a private sphere. But running athwart this outlook is the fact that religious references and invocations continue to play a role in many Western liberal societies. This is particularly relevant in the United States, where the foundations of the Republic were laid partly within a space defined by a religious outlook. The freedom not to be submitted to any human tyrant was seen as given and required by God. The United States self-consciously embraced a public philosophy at its foundation two hundred years ago, one in which religious and biblical themes were prominent. Religion and democratic self-rule were at the outset all but indissolubly linked.

But what can this mean when masses of citizens are no longer believers? Do these Christian or Judeo-Christian references have any more justification? Are they now rather sources of division than of unity? This question smolders underneath virtually all the Western liberal societies, which have emerged from what used to be called Christendom. Even those that are seemingly the most secular in outlook, such as some West European societies, find the problem returning in a new guise, as they begin to incorporate substantial minorities that are neither Christian nor Jewish, but Islamic.

But the United States faces it in a special way, because it is on one hand a Republic self-consciously founded to incorporate freedom, rather than a traditional society that has evolved toward liberalism, as for instance the constitutional monarchies of Europe; while on the other, this foundation was partly couched in religious terms. Perhaps this helps account for the malaise about this issue, which is peculiarly American today.

Liberal and Civic Freedom

Our understanding of the place of religion in a free society is bedeviled by our different understandings of freedom. There are at least two strands in the modern notion that have to be singled out. The first is freedom in the "negative" sense, a condition in which the individual is granted immunity from interference by others in his life, either by state or church or by other individuals. We might call this "liberal" freedom. The second is the freedom we enjoy together to the extent that we govern ourselves as a society and do not live under tutelage or despotism. This could be called "civic" freedom.

Modern democratic societies are founded on the principle that both these freedoms are to be safeguarded. Most of the unfree societies of the modern world deny both. So it is easy to come to believe that they form a kind of "package," whereby each strengthens the other. There is something in this view: of what value is civic freedom if people are not free to speak their minds? And how to ensure the liberal freedoms unless the people have the power to protect them?

But in fact, these two kinds of freedom have been separated in history. Ancient poleis and republics seem strange to us just because they often combined popular rule with very tight control over their members. The sexual mores of citizens were thought to be of public concern in ancient Rome: laxity in this field would ultimately sap citizen virtue. And these societies repeatedly visited exile and confiscation of goods as a penalty on political figures who had fallen out of favor. On the other side, liberal freedoms were expanded under the enlightened despots of the eighteenth century. And many of the educated, advanced thinkers of that age tended to put more faith in a Frederick II or a Catherine the Great to ensure these freedoms, than they did in the will of the uneducated plebs. The vogue of such rulers passed soon afterward, to be sure; and one of the factors that led to its demise was the foundation of America itself. But something of the tension lived on.

94

So in the Macarthyite era in America, it was not surprising that many intellectuals warmed to the "revisionist" or elite theories of democracy, proposed by writers like Joseph Schumpeter.[1] A principal thesis of these was that liberalism, and also governmental efficacy, were better safeguarded when the level and intensity of popular participation in the democratic process were low. These writers tended to be skeptical of, even to pour scorn on, the ideals of civic freedom. In fact, they were more than a little frightened of them.

But the conflict between the two kinds of freedom can also take other forms. It is not just that the civic side may threaten the liberal. It may also be that the very prominence of liberal freedom may undermine the civic. This brings us to a central point that is relevant to the issue of the place of religion, so it is worth while pausing over it a little.

Societies with civic freedom need cohesion. This truth has been repeated over and over again through the long history of political theory. In a despotism, people are constrained to pay their dues to the common good, as conceived by the rulers. They are coerced into obeying the laws, accepting the public disciplines, paying their taxes, even sometimes serving in the armed forces at the risk of their lives. All these things have to be accomplished in a free society as well. Indeed, historically, the burdens of free citizenship have been usually heavier in some crucial respects, since republics generally had citizen armies where despotisms had recourse to mercenaries or professionals. Something then has to replace coercion and fear as the motive for service of the common good in all its forms.

This something has to be a strong sense of commitment to the society, its well-being and survival, on the part of the citizens. This is what Montesquieu called "vertu." It has been a commonplace of the literature on republics since ancient times that without such a spontaneous commitment, public liberty is in danger; the polis may slide toward despotism, as fear and coercion have to come into play to take in the slack. Free societies live on spontaneous cohesion and die for the lack of it. When citizens have to be forced to pay their taxes and defend their homes, despotism is not far off.

This literature may seem rather distant from our present predicament, we who live in large-scale, bureaucratized, technological societies. It may seem to us that only the threat of discovery by the Internal Revenue keeps us paying our taxes, and only conscription, or unemployment, gets us into the armed services. Yet we seem remarkably unruffled by the fear of despotism. But I do not believe that the traditional conceptions are any less applicable today; only the forms have changed.

It is not just that Americans are a little too complacent in their unconcern about despotism; though the reactions to the hearings involving Oliver North in the Iran-Contra scandal were rather troubling in this regard. Rather, it is that there is still a strong sense of commitment to the Republic and what it stands for, and this is a continuing bulwark, even in the teeth of great disaffection and alienation. Thus the way American society and the political system reacted to Watergate, and then the Iran-Contra scandal, shows something very healthy about this society. The ideal that power be controlled by law still means something to masses of people. They can be outraged by its deliberate and premeditated violation, and this is what was translated through the political process into the painstaking investigations that brought the wrongdoing to light. The United States is in this respect still the wonder of the world. Some European and other commentators found the intense and pitiless scrutiny of executive abuses to be excessive, almost pathological. It was taken for a sign of American naïveté, that people here cannot really understand that all governments have to cut certain corners and that things cannot be run any other way.

But in fact, it points to the continuing allegiance of Americans to their own concepts of citizen virtue. And this is something for which the free world ought to be grateful. An American slide into despotism would be horrible to contemplate.

It is not that all free societies have to be as jealous of executive power as the Americans; or rather, since the United States has also invested huge powers in the presidency, one ought to speak of an ambivalence about executive power, one that can at times be crippling. The point has nothing to do with the excellence or absence of it in American institutions. It is rather that the spontaneous cohesion of a free society has to take the form of a common understanding that its political ways and structures are of great value. What takes the place of fear and coercion is a strong sense of common purpose or common value, which by itself can move masses of people to defend or sustain the society. For better or worse, the particular form taken by these common values in the United States incorporates as a central principle this control of power by law. When Americans cease to be concerned about this, it will be a black day for freedom in this country.

Spontaneous cohesion requires common values. Two features of these values should be mentioned here. First, the values have to be common in a strong sense. That means they are not just a convergence of popular judgments and feelings, the kind of thing that might be found out by a poll revealing the popularity of a movie star or a fad for a new kind of therapy. Rather the values are celebrated in common; moreover, integral to our valuing them is the fact that they are celebrated commonly. Thus to cite the example just mentioned, the close control of power by law is certainly a good, one that anyone might value even if they were the last person on earth to do so. But independently of this (and even if the particularly American form of this might be judged excessive, as it is by some Europeans), a great value attaches to the subordination of power to law in the American context precisely because it is one of the focuses for the common valuation by Americans of their political way of life. Part of its value for the individual reposes in its being valued by all.

Second, it is important for freedom that what is commonly valued includes the political system. Any people not totally atomized will have common values; but through much of history, and even today, these may not touch on political matters, and if such values do relate to political matters, they may not exalt the institutions and practices of freedom.

Thus one of the most important focuses of common purpose in the world today is the various forms of nationalism. In some cases, nationalist sentiment can center around language and culture—they galvanize great numbers of people for heroic efforts of liberation or conquest. But they can be terribly destructive of freedom, bringing overwhelming support to structures that are effective at realizing national greatness, even at the risk of despotism. Hitler provided an example of this in the very heart of what we now think of as liberal Europe, though Europe was hardly liberal even prior to Hitler. In other cases, nationalist sentiment may come to crystalize around certain political institutions of a despotic kind, just because these become associated with greatness, as well as with history. I fear that many great Russians have a fondness for the rule of a strong man, probably for reasons such as these. Hence the recurring nostalgia for the age of Stalin, which both astonishes and concerns the foreigner who glimpses it.

In order to serve as a support to freedom, what is commonly valued has to include the institutions and practices of civic freedom. National pride and identification seems to be an indispensable feature of any modern society, but it is a matter of considerable moment that in many liberal democracies the national identity is defined partly in terms of the institutions of political freedom. Political freedom became an important part of English national consciousness as it was forming in the eighteenth century. Political freedom was the starting point for the resistance in the colonies to parliamentary and royal power, the claim that the rights of Englishmen were being denied. When the new republic was formed, it was built self-consciously on the principles of freedom. American patriotism is intrinsically linked with free institutions. This link has found expression in what we often describe as the American "public philosophy."

Even this patriotism can pose a menace to freedom. Figures like Oliver North, and those who admire them, show how an exacerbated and angry national sentiment can, in the end, condone whatever gives it effective outlet, even when that nationalism denies the core values of the society. But the link between national consciousness and the principles of freedom is also what energizes the protests against these violations of the rule of law. Richard M. Nixon would not have been brought so effectively to book if many Americans had not still taken pride in their political institutions.

Now the threat of liberal freedom to civic freedom is indirect but can nevertheless be real. Once negative freedom comes to be seen as the main justification of liberal society, and the main point of an individual's life lies in his following his private plan of life, the common understandings that underpin spontaneous cohesion are given less and less importance. It begins to appear as just another permissible orientation of one's personal life when one is utterly uninterested in politics or the public realm and feels no strong identification with it. So long as one's own plan is conceived and carried out with a sensitivity to the needs of others (under the principle that my freedom stops where I impinge on that of my compatriots), the needs of democracy seem to be met.

In fact, people go on living by common understandings, even when they no longer consciously understand the value of them, even when they come to construe their own life and that of their compatriots in privatistic terms. A crisis like Watergate shows how much these common identifications are still there, under the surface. But by dint of being constantly devalued in a culture of privatistic individualism, and under the weight of a cynical assessment of their relative weakness in modern society, the identifications do risk atrophy. One day, the cynics might prove right, and those who read themselves in atomist terms will actually be right about themselves. The common meanings will be dead. But then liberty will not be in robust health either.

This reflection brings to the fore the basic tension between liberal and civic freedom. The former can accommodate itself very well to a society with virtually no strongly held common values. Indeed, it sometimes seems all the safer in such a society, since there will be nothing there around which a majority might rally to coerce the minority in the name of their common allegiance. But civic freedom cannot long survive the atrophy of such values. Hence those who exclusively value liberal freedom can be tempted to undermine the bases of civic freedom—just as those who place too much value on civic freedom can be highly illiberal.

The Place of Religion

After this long preliminary, the main question can be posed again: what is the place of religion in a free society? If it is liberal freedom we have in mind, it would seem that the negative answer I invoked at the beginning might be the right one. Religion should be free, that is, everybody should be free to profess and practice the religion of their choice, including the null case where this turns out to be no religion at all. But that end seems best served when the state is strictly neutral, meaning when the state is devoid of religion itself and hence when religion has no place in public life.

But the answer may not be the same when we think of civic freedom. This requires some strongly held common values. Can religion be quite absent from them? This is a more vexed question, which does not admit of a one-line answer.

If we consulted ancient tradition, of course, there could be no doubt about the reply. No ancient polis or republic existed in which the religious life was not bound up with the civic. It seemed axiomatic to them that religion must be one with the state. Anything else would threaten to undermine the allegiance of the citizens.

The coming of Christianity made an important change. Christianity started off in an important sense as an antipolitical religion. This is not to say that early Christians opposed political authority. Quite the contrary. But they did not see the political dimension as important in the plan of salvation. They saw government rather as a makeshift, a compensation for our fallen condition, saving us from the worst consequences of the Fall, by at least maintaining order and a minimal peace. This was the outlook, for instance, of Augustine.

Moreover, even where it did not expound a low view of the state, the Christian church gave its members a universal allegiance, which could easily conflict with, or at least rival their political ties. And on top of this, Christianity tended to preach against the warrior virtues, which were often central to the patriotism of early republics. The ideal citizen of an ancient republic was also a warrior.

The result was a certain distance between Christianity and the republican tradition. A writer like Machiavelli, who has to be seen in this light, wondered whether Christianity as against the ancient pagan religions was not an element of potential corruption in a republic. And not only Machiavelli, who might be thought to be specially anti-Christian: Rousseau had similar doubts, although he was more embarrassed about them. From the Christian side, the insistence on some distinction between church and state seemed to render impossible the kind of fusion between polis and religious community that was normal in the ancient world.

The modern world starts with this malaise, which we have not invented in the twentieth century. It is one of the legacies of Christendom that religion can neither be fully integrated in nor fully excluded from the state. But the peculiar modern problem that we have about religion and civic freedom, particularly in America, springs from the beginning of a rapprochement in early modern times between the two. The sense of tension we find in Machiavelli and Rousseau is offset by the rise of a militant Protestantism, in England and Holland, partly allied with traditional institutions in opposition to developing royal absolutism. In the case of the Puritan movements of the English Civil War, the Parliamentary cause begins to be stated in part in terms of the old republican outlook. Milton was a Christian civic humanist.

This new amalgam was of decisive importance for the founding of America. The revolutionary period sees the same mix: a defense of traditional liberties, which takes up the language and concepts of the republican tradition, while at the same time (in New England at least) it is strongly allied with religion. The concept of republican virtue shades over for people like the Adamses into a notion of Christian rectitude, which are seen as alike opposed to the corruptions of irresponsible power that seemed then to dominate the mother country.

This then becomes a crucial part of the consciousness of the new Republic. True, not everyone was on the same wavelength at that time. In particular, one can see an important difference between more or less orthodox Christians, such as were prominent in the revolutionary cause in New England, and the more urbane deists like Jefferson, and even Washington, who took leadership roles in Virginia. This difference was important, as we shall see, but what was quite uncontested at the time was the central place of religious consciousness in the newly defined Republic's life. The core common values were explicitly related to God's purposes for humans, as it is stated, for instance, in the Declaration of Independence, and these were not just stylistic phrases. Tocqueville a few decades later points out the important role that religion plays in American society and in preserving American freedom.

So for all the well-documented tensions between Christianity and the republican tradition, the United States starts its career by linking the two closely together. But if this is so, why at its inception does it introduce the religious liberty clauses? These seem to move toward a separation of religion from the state. They seem to be intended to sideline religion, a first step toward what we seem to experience today, where millions of citizens want to set religion aside altogether as irrelevant to the public sphere.

But to read the religious liberty clauses in this light would be, I believe, profoundly anachronistic. Rather than being part of an attempt to sideline religious consciousness, they aim to remove one of the great obstacles to a meeting of minds on it. The new nation was profoundly diverse in its confessional allegiances. Moreover, many of these denominations had already developed a congregational outlook; that is, they saw themselves not as a church structure that ought to include everyone, but as one fragment of Christendom alongside others—however much they might have disagreed theologically with these others. It is mainly the Anglican church that had wider pretensions, and it of course was the main target of the first and most famous attempt at disestablishment, in Virginia under the leadership of Thomas Jefferson and James Madison.

The religious liberty clauses, which at first bound only the federal government, were meant to prevent any national confessional conformity from being superimposed on the existing diversity. The aim was to prevent full citizenship turning on any particular confessional allegiance, something that would infallibly have alienated a large part of the population. Confessional differences should not stand in the way of anyone's being part of the new Republic and sharing in its common values, including the religious values that were central to it. To the extent that freedom was seen as part of what God destined for humans, one could be playing a part in God's purposes as a citizen outside of any denomination, even as one did as a worshiper in one's particular church. Many Americans could feel related to God in one way through the state, as much as they related to Him in a rather different way through the church congregation.

Of course, this would not be in the forefront of people's minds most of the time. But it comes out in moments of crisis and high significance, as one would expect. Think of the invocations of God on the occasion of great decisions by Abraham Lincoln (and for that matter, by Jefferson Davis) during the Civil War. The God invoked at these moments was a nonconfessional God, no church's property (though sometimes foreigners might feel that He belonged to the Republic). Sometimes we are tempted to think of Him as a deist God. This seems partly justified in virtue of the fact that He was bleached of any particular theology, and that some of His earlier invokers were indeed deist. But this is to make Him blander than He was in fact. Unlike the rather uninvolved deist Creator and rewarder/punisher of the eighteenth century, He had purposes in history, of which American freedom was unquestionably one. The great majority of American Protestants had no difficulty accommodating the God so invoked with the one they worshiped on Sunday in their respective congregations. Catholics had greater problems, but then American Catholicism has been remade by this experience.

Thus the separation of church and state did not have to mean bracketing God or religion. It may have for some, but that is not the way most Americans understood disestablishment. In fact, many supported the measure in the name of religion, to preserve its strength and integrity from the enervating and corrupting effect of state interference. As James Madison put it, "religion and government will both exist in the greater purity, the less they are mixed together."[2]

But many people see it as a bracketing today. That is because this process has become fused in their minds with another, which has also displaced confessional religion from the public domain. This process starts early in the modern period, at the outcome of the first wars of religion. People began to grope toward formulas that would end the senseless killing in the name of God. One way was simply to force conformity with the ruling house, as in the settlement adopted in Germany: *cujos regio, ejus religio*. But in other places where this was not possible, some states began to explore regimes of toleration. These varied greatly from state to state, but their general spirit was to allow the practice of the minority religion as a private affair so long as its followers were loyal citizens in their public life.

Such tolerance leads to the formula that secures peace by relegating religion more and more to the private sphere. Of course, for some centuries still the very thought of a completely lay state was virtually unimaginable. The ruler had to be of some confession or other, and state ritual had to involve ecclesiastics of some church. But people were more and more encouraged in fact to treat this as an affair of the state, something that need have no close connection with whatever living faith the subjects subscribed to. Thomas Hobbes is one of the great theorists of this form of settlement. He tries to show that the ruler has the right to decide questions of public ritual. But in disengaging the subject from the obligation to serve God publicly by his own lights, he implicitly downgrades the importance of this ritual. In return the subject is to be left free to believe what he likes. The really important relation to God now takes place in the private sphere.

This path has been followed in Britain. Disestablishment has never taken place. In fact, there are two established churches in the island. The queen somehow achieves the feat of being head of a Presbyterian Calvinist church in Scotland, and of a broad-spectrum, Catholic-to-Evangelical, Episcopalian church in England. The separation of public from private religion cannot be taken further than that. Over the centuries the various disabilities have been removed from nonmembers of established churches, and the remaining ritual is treated as part of the panoply of the state by virtually everyone, regardless of their belief.

Another perfectly logical end point of this development would be, of course, a lay state, provided this too allowed perfect freedom of (private) religion—something aimed at, for instance, in the French Third Republic.

Let us call these two kinds of displacement of confessional religion from its former dominance respectively, disestablishment and privatization, always bearing in mind that the first term is used very much as a term of art. Processes of privatization may also involve disestablishment in the normal sense of the term, as in France. But in my use of the term I want to focus on the process that occurred in this country, that is, a deconfessionalization that was not a rejection of religion as such from the public sphere.

Most people in modern liberal democracies, particularly those with a secularized outlook, see the entire development of deconfessionalized modern societies in terms of an advancing process of privatization. The step I am calling disestablishment is lost from view, or rather subsumed as a stage in privatization. But this is seriously to distort it, as I have just argued.

The Contemporary Dilemma

But all this might be judged irrelevant to the main question posed here. Of course, historically, privatization was not the only, or even the main, development. But can we adopt any other model today? Surely, it might be thought, in an age where people differ not only in their religious beliefs but in whether one should believe altogether, religion can and must remain a private matter.

If we are concerned only with liberal freedom, this seems an entirely satisfactory answer. Liberal freedoms can accommodate quite well to a neutral state. Or so it is generally believed. But this is because proponents of these freedoms usually picture government as a sort of neutral instrument, serving the converging ends of individuals and arbitrating between them. The important ends and values in life figure, on this view, in the life plans of individuals. The state must have a purely facilitating role, and otherwise has no ends of its own. Indeed, as noted earlier, liberal freedoms seem safer the more neutral and colorless is the state, since there will be less chance that a majority might impose goals on the minority in the name of some supposed common purposes.

But civic freedom cannot accommodate this bleeding of the public domain of all significance. It requires strongly held common values. And we come back to the difficult question: can religion be altogether absent from these?

In order to answer this question properly, it is critical to understand the place of religion in modern life much better. Agnostics often present a picture of linear development, in which more and more people have gradually lost their religious beliefs, culminating in an eventual condition in which religious belief and practice will be a marginal phenomenon. But things do not seem to be turning out that way. For one thing, there seems to be a great deal of lapsing from churches in present-day society that is not matched with a loss of belief in God, in the afterlife, or in some spiritual principle. Deconfessionalization is a major phenomenon, but it by no means betokens simply unbelief. Religion does not decline because churches do. We have only to think of the boom in evangelical Protestant religion now going on in this country. The preachers contact their followers over television or in their own establishments. Some of those who are moved by and subscribe to these preachers may also attend a mainline church, but many others do not. They get their religion as they get everything else in commercial society, delivered where they want it, and against payment. This may be repugnant in certain respects, but it cannot be described in the normal sense as a waning of religion.

But second, even unbelief is not all that it seems. There is a minority of determined atheists who try to construct an entire alternative outlook, but outside of these, there is a broad range of people whose attitudes are more nuanced and ambivalent. In fact, unbelief for most people has not come to fill all the niches in their lives and answer all the questions that religious belief did formerly. This is what is peculiar about the shift to modern secular forms of life, compared with earlier conversions—for example, the rise of Christianity in the Roman Empire or the Islamicization of Asia Minor. Faced with questions about death, about the ultimate meaning of life, about the deepest sources of moral goodness, many people who otherwise think of themselves as secular or agnostic turn to the religion from which they or their family emerged. Or groping for a language to mark or celebrate the crucial moments in life, such as birth, marriage, and death, they can only find it in the old faiths. For the hard-bitten atheists, these are lapses, regrettable moments of weakness, where the need for austere courage in the face of the dark and meaningless universe is forgotten. That is undoubtedly one way of reading these phenomena, but it is very far removed from the way the people concerned often understand them.

In any case, whatever the reason, the turn away from religion is a much more partial and ambivalent thing than we usually think. Some religious reading of ultimate questions remains alive for many people who seem otherwise to have dropped out altogether. This is what makes it difficult to exclude religion from public space.

One possible way to do this is by means of a militantly lay philosophy of political society, as we see in the French republican tradition. This tries to attain civic freedom within an explicit set of common values and symbols that are defined as non- or even antireligious. This solution has the advantage of facing head-on the problem of how to have vibrant common purposes without religion. But there has clearly been a cost. In the French case, it was a century and a half of political division, almost latent civil war. Vichy finally so discredited the Catholic right that this division was ended. But with the demise of one combatant, the other starts to weaken as well. Militant laicism is also on the wane in France, as the recent socialist attempt to cut back on the largely Catholic "écoles libres" showed. The attempt to exclude the religious still leaves lots of people cold.

Where the lay philosophy has not been made the basis of the state, people's natural ambivalence is allowed free rein. In moments of crisis or great peril, it seems natural to invoke God. Even Stalin was induced to reestablish the Patriarchate in Moscow when faced with Nazi invasion. This parallels the bereaved individual's recourse, say, to a religious funeral for parent or spouse.

This comes about all the easier in societies that are held together by a sense of long-lasting national tradition, in which historically certain religious forms have played an undeniable role. This is the case, for instance, in England with the Anglican church. In fact most of those who practice some religion do not belong to it, and most of those who nominally belong to it do not practice any religion. But it is unquestionably bound up with the history of England and her monarchs, and so the whole nation can enjoy the pageantry of a royal wedding in St. Paul's Cathedral, Anglicans presumably in one way, dissenters, Catholics, Jews, and agnostics in diverse other ways. Those whom the invocation of God leaves cold may be moved by display of centuries-old tradition.

But these solutions do not fit the United States. This is a country whose common values were from the beginning organized around certain defined ideas, understandings of freedom: what has been described as a "public philosophy." It is a country, moreover, where the crucial inner battles, in particular the literal and bloody struggle of the Civil War, were fought in the name of interpretations of this philosophy. It is entirely in keeping with this tradition—to put it somewhat paradoxically—that Americans should not be satisfied just with the forms that are handed down but should seek to redefine them in the light of their contemporary understandings of the foundational ideas. American unbelievers are uneasy before the American equivalents of the coronation in Westminster Abbey, or the wedding in St. Paul's Cathedral. Someone could argue about prayer in school, for instance, that (in suitably undenominational form) it was an utterly natural part of the earlier conception of what America was about; that it fits admirably with the language in which the Declaration of Independence is couched and with their status as one people "under God." But to many Americans it seems truer to these founding acts to challenge this practice of prayer, since however undenominational, it could not include those who believe that there is no one to pray to. Even the ultimate in reduced content, a minute of silence, has been argued against in one case.

Being a nation founded on ideas, Americans often demand that their contemporary understanding of these be given precedence over respect and celebration of the historical forms they have taken. This can seem unreasonable to Britons, and it must also be said, Canadians, but there is no doubt that it has warrant in the American way.

This seems to open the path to a French solution, a redefinition of national purpose in lay terms. But this is not easy to accomplish either. The original nonconfessional theism still resonates with many Americans. To excise God is to eviscerate the common purpose, as they understand it. Partly because of their substantive beliefs, and partly out of historical piety, the original forms are still cherished by millions of Americans.

We have the makings here of another American dilemma, one that is now rather low level, because not much energy is invested in it, but which could escalate into a "Kulturkampf." By Kulturkampf, I mean something more serious than disputes about school prayer or aid to schools; I mean (as in the original German case) a struggle about the place of religion in public life, in which at least one side challenges the very legitimacy of the other's position and is willing to brand it as utterly alien to the American way.

In a situation where the population is more and more diverse, in which many do not believe in any religion, and growing numbers belong to religions outside the Judeo-Christian tradition, there is an obvious temptation to take religion right out of the public domain. If America were concerned simply with liberal freedoms, and were willing to confide these to a neutral and merely instrumental state, in a public domain stripped of moral prestige, this would be a viable solution. But America is also about civic freedom, and it is a very real question whether even liberal freedoms would be safe where they are not guaranteed by a political system that enshrines common purposes still held in reverence by the citizens. In a merely instrumental state, bled of its moral significance, people would no longer be shocked by Watergate, and then all kinds of liberty would be less secure.

But in a political system founded on common values, which had moreover their earlier canonical expression in religious terms, it is very hard just to take the road of privatization and declare religion altogether outside the public domain. If it should come to a Kulturkampf, it is clear that neither side could win. Nor would either side unequivocally deserve to.

It might be thought that the solution, after all, lies at hand. If Americans can find a modus vivendi when they think in terms of liberal freedom, but they need some strong common purposes as the bulwarks even of this freedom, why can't they make liberalism itself the common purpose? The American way, as a way of freedom, would now be defined as the system in which the individual liberty of each is respected by all. Giving space for the individual would now be the inspiring common purpose. And this, after all, is one of the obvious things that differentiates this country from despotisms the world over, of left or right.

I think many Americans do see their country in this light today. This view gives one a positive reason to bleach religion from public space, precisely in order to avoid any hint of restriction of access that might cramp the prospects of unbelieving compatriots. And it seems to give an answer to the dilemma of how to keep vibrant public purposes in the absence of religion. This form of liberalism is not militantly lay: religious people can also subscribe to it for their own reasons, but it is at the same time not tied to any religious outlook.

This solution, variants of which are defended by some of the best minds in American political and legal theory,[3] may work pragmatically; that is, it may be accepted by enough people to muffle the potential conflict. But there are several things wrong with it. First, it involves sidelining altogether civic freedom. But this is already in danger of being forgotten in contemporary America, which is tending to emphasize more and more the recovery of rights and less and less the good of participation as the core of citizen dignity.[4] And second, there is a strange pragmatic contradiction at the core of this position. Common purposes are only sustained to the extent that people do not identify themselves exclusively as individuals but also see themselves at least in part as essentially defined by their adherence to the political community. Common as against merely convergent goods by their very definition must be "ours" as against simply mine and yours and his and hers, severally. The common understanding of our way of life as sustaining liberal freedom would be in its situation in our lives a common purpose. But what it exalts as valuable is exclusively individual self-fulfillment, plus relations of fairness between these self-directing individuals. It offers a picture of human life in which common purposes have no valid place, in which they appear more often as potential obstacles to individual self-development. Indeed, what one finds where the culture of liberalism is strong is that the possibility of genuinely common values gets lost from sight. A kind of philosophical atomism becomes widespread by which all public enterprises are construed as based on merely convergent purposes. The alternative is occluded and falls outside the range of imagined human possibilities. This is certainly the case with mainstream philosophy and social science in this country.

The contradiction holds thus between the life situation of this view, as a genuinely common purpose, and what it affirms and defines as good. Of course, if its only problem were a species of philosophical inconsistency, we might safely ignore it as irrelevant for political life. But in fact, this inconsistency both reflects and abets a movement of culture toward a kind of atomistic individualism, concerned exclusively with self-fulfillment. And this in turn threatens to undermine the genuinely common purposes in this society, at all levels: the familial and community as well as the political. The intellectual inconsistency reflects and facilitates an actual self-undermining of this form of liberalism, which tends to sap the sources of its own political strength.[5]

But if we set this aside, it is not easy to see an intellectually coherent and politically effective solution to this dilemma in contemporary America. One can hope that the struggle remain at a low level of intensity. Pragmatically, there is not much difference in America around two of the three main implications of any separation of church and state. These are to avoid all exclusions of citizens from the public process or opportunities on grounds of religious differences, to avoid any coerced support by citizens of religious forms they do not adhere to, as often happens with an established church, and to define symbols and forms of expression that all can recognize themselves in.

It would appear that the first and second are uncontroversial as principles in all Western democracies. And in addition, there does not seem to be a great deal of division about their application. There have been objections to certain practices, for example, publicly supported display of religious symbols, on grounds of the second principle; but one might surmise that what really animates the protest is something like the third principle, since the degree of support here has been materially trivial and the symbols not offensive.

Much of the future course of this issue of religion in public life will hinge on whether Americans are happy with a high score on the first and second, or whether they feel they have to grasp the nettle of the third principle. In a way, this is a difficult thing to avoid in America, because the British solution of common recognition in historical symbols as historical seems less strong here than the drive to give expression to contemporary understanding of the core ideas around which the Republic was built. And there are good reasons in American political culture why this is likely to continue. And perhaps it should continue, for the health of the Republic.

But the issue is complicated on the American scene by the fact that, beyond the three principal objectives I have just outlined, American jurisprudence has interpreted the no establishment clause as a commitment to eschew all public support to religious bodies. This might perhaps be a simple enough principle to apply if it concerned only government relations to churches. But with the existence of institutions not easily classifiable, like sectarian schools, it opens a quagmire for public policy, from which it has been impossible to extricate the law with any semblance of intellectual coherence and consistency. Thus, for example, remedial reading lessons for dyslexic children by public school teachers, but in parochial schools, is ineligible for state support, while governments can give tax breaks to parents to cover tuition at such schools.[6] People on both sides of these issues feel unreconciled to these judgments, and the more so because there does not seem to be any defensible intellectual principle underlying them.

Even so, if a pragmatic sense of the importance of the first and second objectives were the underlying common motive, it ought to be possible to resolve most of these issues in a satisfactory way. The difficulty seems to be that in the United States the "wall of separation" has itself become a symbol. Adjudication on these questions is carried out, emotionally if not intellectually, in the ambit of the third objective.

To the extent that this is so, the outlook is rather pessimistic because this issue threatens to be the occasion of a Kulturkampf, which cannot find an easy solution. If what I just called the "liberal solution" is inadequate, and if the "British solution" is unviable, then there does not seem to be another honorable and practical compromise, let alone one that can shine consistently through all the Byzantine detail of government's relation to the school system. Of course, this is not a prediction. All sorts of things might happen: Americans might end up being satisfied with a high score on the first and second principles; the liberal solution might work politically, for all its intellectual incoherence.

But if all these break down, and a Kulturkampf threatens, perhaps the reflections offered here might be of some help. That is, these reflections might contribute to mitigating the conflict if the protagonists of both sides could grasp the nature of the dilemma, and behind this, of the whole complex and ambivalent place of religion in modern culture. One of the difficulties now is the widespread belief on both sides that there is a perfectly coherent and honorable compromise, that is, the one that they respectively support—and which each attributes to the original framers. For some, America is founded on a certain religious vision, and one departs from the common purpose in wanting to exclude God from the public realm. For others, there is an obvious liberal solution based on respecting different private choices in this matter, and those who resist this are illiberal and go against the American way. The very nature of a Kulturkampf resides in this certainty that only one solution is defensible.

This blindness to the complexity of the case is particularly striking among the liberals because they are often more educated, more learned, and more sophisticated than their opponents but frequently no less dogmatic and unyielding. Liberal American intellectuals tend to be extraordinarily blind to the force of religion even in their own lives, let alone in those of their compatriots. On the other side, proponents of the Christian right are often ready to indulge in crude conspiracy theories that utterly caricature the deeply felt convictions of their more secular-minded neighbors. If one could get beyond this—for example, in the direction taken by the Williamsburg Charter—the conflict might be transformed. A struggle in which each could understand something of the force of the other's response to a common dilemma would virtually by definition be proof against degenerating into a Kulturkampf.

Perhaps there is a hope in this direction, not only for mutual understanding, but for a revivifying of the public sphere. Some of the acerbity of the present debate comes from the sense on both sides that the public philosophy of the United States may be less cherished and less widely recognized among its citizens than in the past. So that each feels an urgent need to press its variant of this philosophy all the stronger. But an honest recognition on both sides of the dilemmas, and the consequent acknowledgement by each of the good faith of the other, could lead to the recognition that it is part of the public philosophy of America that this very philosophy should be a matter of continuing discussion and debate. So it was in the beginning in matters of federal economic power, so it was later in issues of states' rights and slavery, and so it is today. The extraordinary strength of America comes from the ability of its people to continue and sustain debates over fundamental matters without flying apart into warring factions. Breakdown did occur in 1861, as perhaps it had to over an issue as deep and searing as slavery. But it need not today. A debate whose legitimacy was acknowledged by both sides could make the sense of commitment to a common public philosophy come alive for millions of Americans. While a Kulturkampf waged by blinkered minorities would just accelerate the slide into privatization on the part of the alienated majority. Paradoxically, a pressing danger can be turned into a source of hope.

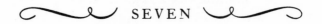

SEVEN

Afterword

PETER L. BERGER

IN RECENT DISCUSSIONS of the place of religious liberty in the American polity a number of people have argued that religious liberty is the first liberty, that it is the foundation, the *fons et origo,* of all the other rights and liberties. I for one agree with the basic proposition, and I do so for one, overridingly important reason—the polity that recognizes religious liberty as a fundamental human right thereby recognizes (knowingly or unknowingly) the limits of political power.

It is easy enough to see why this should be so. At the core of man's religious quest is the experience of transcendence, the encounter with a reality that is "totally other" than all the realities of ordinary life. And a necessary consequence of this encounter is that all the ordinary realities, including the most imposing and oppressive ones, are relativized. In the realm of human institutions, none is the more imposing and (at least potentially) more oppressive than the polity, especially in its recent embodiment as the modern state, which is a historically unprecedented agglomeration of power. This characteristic, of course, is manifested most terrifyingly in the modern totalitarian state, but all contemporary states, even the most democratic ones, possess instruments of power that would have made the most awesome tyrants of antiquity green with envy. (Think of what Genghis Khan could have done with radio communications, or the Emperor Caligula with an internal revenue service!) The state is very serious business indeed, deadly business (for in the end every state, even the most peaceful one, rests on the power of the sword), and those who represent the state take themselves very seriously. That is why the state always wraps itself in religious or quasi-religious symbols, why it fosters solemn ceremonies, and why the refusal to be serious about the state is everywhere a punishable offense (from *lese-majeste* to contempt of Congress). Given all this, it should not surprise us that there is a built-in tension between all institutions of political power and the religious quest that tends toward relativizing them.

This has always been so. The holders of political power have always tried to contain the potentially subversive force of religion by controlling religious institutions. Most of the time they have been successful in this, but ever again there appeared religious spokesmen—emissaries of transcendence, if you will—who refused to play the roles of legitimators of the political status quo. The power-holders naturally took a very dim view of these troublemakers and frequently enough they employed very disagreeable methods to deal with them. The more tyrannical the ruler, the more urgent was the need to shut up the troublemakers.

In the biblical tradition, of course, the figure of the prophet most clearly represents this religious challenge to the self-important seriousness of the rulers of this world—prototypically, in the confrontation between Nathan and King David. This drama of speaking transcendent truth to worldly power has been reenacted many times in the history of Judaism, Christianity, and Islam, the three great streams flowing out of the biblical experience. It should be stressed, though, that comparable relativizations of the polity occurred in other traditions. The figures of Antigone and Socrates embody it in classical antiquity, as do a long line of Hindu sages, Buddhist monks, and Confucian scholars. All human religions are windows on the vastness of the transcendent: open any one of these windows, and the glitter of political power suddenly reveals itself to be a rather shabby affair.

It is precisely in this quality of relativizing, unmasking, debunking the pretensions of human power that we can see the deep affinity between the religious and the comic, between the prophet and the clown. The prophet proclaims that God laughs at all the kings and emperors of the earth; the clown makes a joke and reveals that the emperor has no clothes. No wonder, then, that tyrants are afraid of prophecy and of jokes. No wonder that the tyrants of modern totalitarianism, very logically, have been equally assiduous in controlling the institutions that (heaven forbid) may bring forth prophets as they have been in persecuting anyone who dared to make jokes about their grimly serious agendas. And this is why churches have become the last refuge of dissenters in all totalitarian societies, and why the same societies have produced a luxurious growth of underground humor.

Eastern Europe, I suppose, has been the most fertile ground for this kind of relativizing (and, in the deepest sense of the word, redeeming) humor.—It is the year 2088. Two Czechs are standing on St. Wenceslas Square in Prague, in front of the Lumumba monument. There is a long silence, and then one says to the other: "You know, it was better under the Chinese."

There was the man who walked into a state department store in Leipzig and asked for undershirts. The salesperson told him, "You have to go to the third floor. There they have no undershirts. On this floor we have no shirts." Some readers may know the Soviet stories about the mythical radio station in Erivan to which listeners may send questions. Question to Radio Erivan: "Is it not true that the Soviet government governs much better than did the Tsarist government?" Radio Erivan answers: "Yes, of course." Question: "Yet it seems that the Tsarist government was more popular. Why is that?" Answer: "Because it governed less." When people laugh at such jokes in Prague or in Leningrad it is as if, for one joyful moment, the prison walls of the totalitarian society are breached, transcended (precisely), and there is a whiff of the fresh air of freedom. And (whatever the differences between these experiences) this is just what happens as people gather in barely tolerated churches and synagogues to worship a God who is more powerful than all the tyrants of this world.

A believing Jew or Christian can put this insight into a theological proposition: redemption will one day be perceived as an immense comic relief, and even now, in an as-yet-unredeemed world, redemption can be anticipated as a healing joke. Yet I am certain that my view about the primacy of religious liberty in a catalogue of liberties would remain the same if tomorrow I should lose my faith and should redefine myself as an agnostic. As an agnostic I would also be concerned that human existence not be confined in the prison of ordinary reality, and even if I would now be unable to make positive affirmations about the nature of that which transcends our ordinary lives, I would not want steel bars to be imposed on every window that might, conceivably, open up on unthought-of possibilities. In other words, there is a secular argument to be made for the primacy of religious liberty, as there are secular reasons for the democratic option against the totalitarian temptations of our age.

This points us to a paradox, which is particularly relevant to current debates over the meaning of the First Amendment in the United States. Without going into constitutional and juridical ramifications of this issue, it seems to me that there is a depressing triviality about much that has been said about a "secular purpose" in this or that activity of religious institutions, including some things that have been said by the Supreme Court. (We need not dwell here on the remarkable spectacle of these nine characters, swishing around in priestly robes in a building resembling a Greek temple and engaged in the endless exegesis of a sacred text—and then having the chutzpah of insisting that there is no establishment of religion in America.) To be sure, there is a "secular purpose" served if a church runs a soup kitchen, an orphanage, or even (though this is more doubtful) a university. But the most important secular purpose any church can serve is to remind people that there is a meaning to human existence that transcends all worldly agendas, that all human institutions (including the nation-state) are only relatively important and are ultimately not to be taken seriously, and that all worldly authority (even that of the Supreme Court of the United States) is disclosed to be comically irrelevant in the perspective of transcendence.

Here, then, is the paradox: religious institutions serve their most important secular purpose precisely when they are least secular in their activities. Society, under certain circumstances, can easily dispense with church-operated soup kitchens or universities. Society can ill afford to lose the reminders of transcendence that the church provides every time it worships God. The protection of religious liberty serves the purpose of this ultimate anamnesis, which ipso facto protects the possibility of laughter and the wondrous mystery of the human condition.

I do not share the view that democracy is the noblest form of government, even less the Wilsonian messianism that would see the United States as the providential instrument by which democracy is to be imposed on every nation on earth (a messianism, incidentally, to which the American right is as prone as the American left—the two only differ as to which recalcitrant countries are to be the objects of the democratic crusade). Rather, I am inclined to agree with Winston Churchill that democracy is an appalling business—until one considers the alternatives—or at least those that are available under modern conditions. The modern state, for reasons rooted in its very structure, contains the impulse to expand into every nook and cranny of society. The totalitarian state is, of course, the apotheosis (I choose the word deliberately) of this impulse.

Democracy provides the only half-way reliable institutional mechanisms to curb the totalitarian impulse. It does not do this because of its ideology: As J. L. Talmon has convincingly shown, there is such a thing as "totalitarian democracy," at least in the sphere of ideas (Jacobin in its original version), sometimes (alas) in the sphere of facts. But the core of Western democracy, and certainly of the democratic experiment of the United States, is the institutionalization of limits on the power of government. Political scientists have defined democracy in different ways; most come down to two key elements—regular elections and some sort of bill of rights. In other words, democracy seeks to ensure (not sporadically, but through predictable institutions) that the rascals can be thrown out from time to time and that there are certain things that they cannot do while they are in.

Democracy (not as an idea, but as a functioning political reality) is based on suspicion and irreverence—which is precisely why it is the best shield against the totalitarian project, which demands faith and veneration. Any democratic constitution must say to the state, repetitively and insistently, "Thus far, and no farther!" Every protection of political liberties and of human rights, of course, does just that. The recognition of religious liberty, as a fundamental and irrevocable right, does it in a fundamental way. Religious liberty is not one of many benefits that the state may choose to bestow on its subjects; rather, religious liberty is rooted in the very nature of man and, when the state recognizes it, the state ipso facto bows before a sovereignty that radically transcends every worldly manifestation of power. For the religious believer, of course, this is the sovereignty of God; for the agnostic it will be the sovereignty of that mystery within man that ever thrives to go beyond the given—the mystery of man's freedom.

These considerations have very practical implications for many of the controversies currently dividing American society. We have reason to be grateful that this society is democratically governed, that controversy is possible and indeed protected, and that by and large religious liberty is secure. However, it would be very foolish to overlook the totalitarian tendencies even within this society, some of them very much present in issues touching on religious liberty. I do not have the time to spell this out; suffice it to say that one of the hallmarks of the totalitarian project is always the urge to drive underground the metaphysical propensity in man, to banish transcendence from the public square (except in the domesticated form of established or civil religion), and to make all of social life subject to the trivial worldview of functional rationality. Put simply, the totalitarian project requires a world without windows; the defense of religious liberty is the counterproject of keeping alive a sense of the wonder of our condition.

But how does fundamentalism fit into this picture? The problem, of course, is that one man's fundamentalism is another's self-evident truth. Depending on where you happen to live, the word may evoke Communist Party officials trying to preserve Marxist-Leninist orthodoxy, ayatollahs putting women behind veils, or born-again seminary trustees firing professors for not teaching that Moses wrote the Pentateuch. I happen to live two blocks from the Charles River; when I hear the word "fundamentalism," I think of my academic colleagues and neighbors whose unbending convictions and self-righteous intolerance of heretics are fully up to ayatollah standards (though, thank God, they lack ayatollah means of enforcement). Perhaps we can be satisfied here with an ad hoc definition of fundamentalism as any all-embracing system of belief held with rigid certitude and coupled with the moral assurance of one's right to impose it on everyone else. Fundamentalism thus understood, whatever its ideational content, will always be an enemy of religious liberty; always and everywhere, it can only flourish behind tightly shut windows; and wherever it sees an open window, it is under the urgent compulsion to slam it shut.

It is undoubtedly correct to say that, through most of human history, the content of most fundamentalisms has been religious. The reasons can be explained, but this coincidence between religion and fanaticism must be a source of sorrow for any religious believer. It is a source of sorrow for me since I believe that not only is it possible to be religious without being fanatical, but that genuine religious faith precludes fanaticism. In the contemporary world too, sad to say, there has been a notable upsurge of religious fundamentalisms. The most dramatic cases of this, of course, are Islamic and Protestant fundamentalism, both enormously powerful forces cross-nationally and both (though there are very important differences between them) capable of inspiring large numbers of people to make radical changes in their lives. Other religious traditions, however, have shown themselves capable of very similar outbursts of unlovely and at times homicidal fanaticism. Let me just mention both Catholics and Protestants in Northern Ireland, every sect of Islam and Christianity in Lebanon, Jewish fundamentalists in Israel, both Hindus and Buddhists in Sri Lanka, Sikhs in the Punjab, and an odd assortment of syncretistic cults all across sub-Saharan Africa.

Those who regard Protestant fundamentalism in this country as constituting a comparable danger to pluralism and to civic peace are unconvincing, but let it be stipulated that there are situations in America too where religious liberty is threatened by religious fanaticism (I would certainly think so if I were a seminary professor about to be fired for teaching modern methods of biblical scholarship, though, even in my distress, I would console myself with the knowledge that my persecutors cannot call upon the police to assist them).

All the same, it seems to me that the most pervasive fundamentalisms facing us here are secular ones. Politically, they are both of the left and the right. In the milieu of the "new knowledge class" in America, it would be unnecessary to go on about the right (as when, in an act he himself modestly described as one of courage, the former president of Yale University denounced the Moral Majority—at Yale). In this milieu there is bemused contempt about the "superstitions" of religious fundamentalists, such as their belief that the Bible is literally inspired or that prayer can cause miracles.

As a theologically liberal Lutheran, I must confess that I find the first proposition very improbable and that I am inclined to skepticism about any concrete specification of the second. But among the cultured despisers of Jerry Falwell and his cohorts it is widely believed that the Soviet Union has changed fundamentally because it has the first leader with clothes that fit, that the establishment of racial quotas is a means toward a race-blind society, or that a six-month fetus should have a legal status roughly comparable to a wart. It seems to me that here we have "superstitions" greatly more dangerous than those found in the Protestant hinterland. It is the values and prejudices of the knowledge class, not those of the Reverend Jerry Falwell, that today shape important policies, are enacted into law, and define what is culturally acceptable. It is primarily against them, and not against the subculture of conservative Protestantism, that religious liberty must be protected. It is precisely the knowledge class that today seeks an "establishment of religion"–that is, the imposition through state power of its particular worldview and morality—and which interferes with the "free exercise of religion" of those who disagree with its ideology.

The social psychology of all fundamentalisms, religious or secular, holds no great enigmas. Its core motive is what Erich Fromm called the "escape from freedom"–the flight into an illusionary and necessarily intolerant certitude from the insecurities of being human. In all likelihood this motive is age old, but it takes on a special force under the circumstances of modernity. Indeed there would seem to be a dialectical relation between the multiplication of choices brought about by modern pluralism and the flight into a once-and-for-all choice posited as an absolute. The affirmation of religious liberty, by contrast, is finally grounded in the refusal to participate in this flight into fanaticism. Once again, it can take a religious or a secular form: the latter will be a stoic acceptance of uncertainty; the former is based on the recognition that faith does not require false certitudes, that it can even live with doubt. This is why the fanatic cannot laugh (an incapacity he shares with the totalitarian); faith, on the other hand, opens up the possibility of laughter at the most profound level—the laughter that participates, in anticipation, in the joyful play of the angels.

 APPENDIX

The Williamsburg Charter

A Word about the Williamsburg Charter

The Williamsburg Charter was written and published expressly to address the dilemmas, challenges, and opportunities posed by religious liberty in American public life today. Beginning in the fall of 1986, the charter was drafted by representatives of American leading faiths—Protestant, Catholic, Jewish, and secularist in particular. It was revised over the course of two years in close consultation with political leaders, scholars from many disciplines, and leaders from a wide array of faith communities. Named after Williamsburg in honor of the city's role as the cradle of religious liberty in America, it was presented to the nation in Williamsburg on June 25, 1988, when the first one hundred national signers signed it publicly on the occasion of the 200th anniversary of Virginia's call for the Bill of Rights.

The stated purpose of the charter is fourfold: to celebrate the uniqueness of the First Amendment religious liberty clauses; to reaffirm religious liberty—or freedom of conscience—for citizens of all faiths and none; to set out the place of religious liberty within American public life; and to define the guiding principles by which people with deep differences can contend robustly but civilly in the public arena.

There are three main sections in the charter: first, a call for a reaffirmation of the first principles that underlie the religious liberty in American experience; second, a call for a reappraisal of the course and conduct of recent public controversies; and third, a call for "reconstitution" of the American people, in the sense of this generation reappropriating the framers' vision and ideals in our time.

Numerous individual points could be highlighted in a document that has much to say on current issues in law and society—the place accorded to naturalistic faiths, the delineation of the relationship of the two religious liberty clauses, the mention of the menace of the modern state, the insistence on the danger of "semi-establishments," and so on. But the two principal themes of the charter center on the importance of religious liberty as America's "first liberty," and on the religious liberty clauses as the "golden rule" for civic life. These themes—the inalienable right and the universal duty to respect that right—are developed in various ways, ranging from exposition of first principles to contemporary guidelines, but the overall effect is a powerful restatement of a critical aspect of America's public philosophy.

The Williamsburg Charter

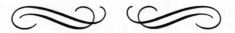

KEENLY AWARE of the high national purpose of commemorating the bicentennial of the United States Constitution, we who sign this Charter seek to celebrate the Constitution's greatness, and to call for a bold reaffirmation and reappraisal of its vision and guiding principles. In particular, we call for a fresh consideration of religious liberty in our time, and of the place of the First Amendment Religious Liberty clauses in our national life.

We gratefully acknowledge that the Constitution has been hailed as America's "chief export" and "the most wonderful work ever struck off at a given time by the brain and purpose of man." Today, two hundred years after its signing, the Constitution is not only the world's oldest, still-effective written constitution, but the admired pattern of ordered liberty for countless people in many lands.

In spite of its enduring and universal qualities, however, some provisions of the Constitution are now the subject of widespread controversy in the United States. One area of intense controversy concerns the First Amendment Religious Liberty clauses, whose mutually reinforcing provisions act as a double guarantee of religious liberty, one part barring the making of any law "respecting an establishment of religion" and the other barring any law "prohibiting the free exercise thereof."

The First Amendment Religious Liberty provisions epitomize the Constitution's visionary realism. They were, as James Madison said, the "true remedy" to the predicament of religious conflict they originally addressed, and they well express the responsibilities and limits of the state with respect to liberty and justice.

Our commemoration of the Constitution's bicentennial must therefore go beyond celebration to rededication. Unless this is done, an irreplaceable part of national life will be endangered, and a remarkable opportunity for the expansion of liberty will be lost.

For we judge that the present controversies over religion in public life pose both a danger and an opportunity. There is evident danger in the fact that certain forms of politically reassertive religion in parts of the world are, in principle, enemies of democratic freedom and a source of deep social antagonism. There is also evident opportunity in the growing philosophical and cultural awareness that all people live by commitments and ideals, that value-neutrality is impossible in the ordering of society, and that we are on the edge of a promising moment for a fresh assessment of pluralism and liberty. It is with an eye to both the promise and the peril that we publish this Charter and pledge ourselves to its principles.

We readily acknowledge our continuing differences. Signing this Charter implies no pretense that we believe the same things or that our differences over policy proposals, legal interpretations and philosophical groundings do not ultimately matter. The truth is not even that what unites us is deeper than what divides us, for differences over belief are the deepest and least easily negotiated of all.

The Charter sets forth a renewed national compact, in the sense of a solemn mutual agreement between parties, on how we view the place of religion in American life and how we should contend with each other's deepest differences in the public sphere. It is a call to a vision of public life that will allow conflict to lead to consensus, religious commitment to reinforce political civility. In this way, diversity is not a point of weakness but a source of strength.

A TIME FOR REAFFIRMATION

We believe, in the first place, that the nature of the Religious Liberty clauses must be understood before the problems surrounding them can be resolved. We therefore affirm both their cardinal assumptions and the reasons for their crucial national importance.

With regard to the assumptions of the First Amendment Religious Liberty clauses, we hold three to be chief:

The Inalienable Right

Nothing is more characteristic of humankind than the natural and inescapable drive toward meaning and belonging, toward making sense of life and finding community in the world. As fundamental and precious as life itself, this "will to meaning" finds expression in ultimate beliefs, whether theistic or non-theistic, transcendent or naturalistic, and these beliefs are most our own when a matter of conviction rather than coercion. They are most our own when, in the words of George Mason, the principal author of the Virginia Declaration of Rights, they are "directed only by reason and conviction, not by force or violence."

As James Madison expressed it in his Memorial and Remonstrance, "The Religion then of every man must be left to the conviction and conscience of every man; and it is the right of every man to exercise it as these may dictate. This right is in its nature an unalienable right."

Two hundred years later, despite dramatic changes in life and a marked increase of naturalistic philosophies in some parts of the world and in certain sectors of our society, this right to religious liberty based upon freedom of conscience remains fundamental and inalienable. While particular beliefs may be true or false, better or worse, the right to reach, hold, exercise them freely, or change them, is basic and non-negotiable.

Religious liberty finally depends on neither the favors of the state and its officials nor the vagaries of tyrants or majorities. Religious liberty in a democracy is a right that may not be submitted to vote and depends on the outcome of no election. A society is only as just and free as it is respectful of this right, especially toward the beliefs of its smallest minorities and least popular communities.

The right to freedom of conscience is premised not upon science, nor upon social utility, nor upon pride of species. Rather, it is premised upon the inviolable dignity of the human person. It is the foundation of, and is integrally related to, all other rights and freedoms secured by the Constitution. This basic civil liberty is clearly acknowledged in the Declaration of Independence and is ineradicable from the long tradition of rights and liberties from which the Revolution sprang.

The Ever Present Danger

No threat to freedom of conscience and religious liberty has historically been greater than the coercions of both Church and State. These two institutions—the one religious, the other political—have through the centuries succumbed to the temptation of coercion in their claims over minds and souls. When these institutions and their claims have been combined, it has too often resulted in terrible violations of human liberty and dignity. They are so combined when the sword and purse of the State are in the hands of the Church, or when the State usurps the mantle of the Church so as to coerce the conscience and compel belief. These and other such confusions of religion and state authority represent the misordering of religion and government which it is the purpose of the Religious Liberty provisions to prevent.

Authorities and orthodoxies have changed, kingdoms and empires have come and gone, yet as John Milton once warned, "new Presbyter is but old priest writ large." Similarly, the modern persecutor of religion is but ancient tyrant with more refined instruments of control. Moreover, many of the greatest crimes against conscience of this century have been committed, not by religious authorities, but by ideologues virulently opposed to traditional religion.

Yet whether ancient or modern, issuing from religion or ideology, the result is the same: religious and ideological orthodoxies, when politically established, lead only too naturally toward what Roger Williams called a "spiritual rape" that coerces the conscience and produces "rivers of civil blood" that stain the record of human history.

Less dramatic but also lethal to freedom and the chief menace to religious liberty today is the expanding power of government control over personal behavior and the institutions of society, when the government acts not so much in deliberate hostility to, but in reckless disregard of, communal belief and personal conscience.

Thanks principally to the wisdom of the First Amendment, the American experience is different. But even in America where state-established orthodoxies are unlawful and the state is constitutionally limited, religious liberty can never be taken for granted. It is a rare achievement that requires constant protection.

The Most Nearly Perfect Solution

Knowing well that "nothing human can be perfect" (James Madison) and that the Constitution was not "a faultless work" (Gouverneur Morris), the Framers nevertheless saw the First Amendment as a "true remedy" and the most nearly perfect solution yet devised for properly ordering the relationship of religion and the state in a free society.

There have been occasions when the protections of the First Amendment have been overridden or imperfectly applied. Nonetheless, the First Amendment is a momentous decision for religious liberty, the most important political decision for religious liberty and public justice in the history of humankind. Limitation upon religious liberty is allowable only where the State has borne a heavy burden of proof that the limitation is justified—not by any ordinary public interest, but by a supreme public necessity—and that no less restrictive alternative to limitation exists.

The Religious Liberty clauses are a brilliant construct in which both No establishment and Free exercise serve the ends of religious liberty and freedom of conscience. No longer can sword, purse and sacred mantle be equated. Now, the government is barred from using religion's mantle to become a confessional State, and from allowing religion to use the government's sword and purse to become a coercing Church. In this new order, the freedom of the government from religious control and the freedom of religion from government control are a double guarantee of the protection of rights. No faith is preferred or prohibited, for where there is no state-definable orthodoxy, there can be no state-punishable heresy.

With regard to the reasons why the First Amendment Religious Liberty clauses are important for the nation today, we hold five to be preeminent:

The First Amendment Religious Liberty provisions have both a logical and historical priority in the Bill of Rights. They have logical priority because the security of all rights rests upon the recognition that they are neither given by the state, nor can they be taken away by the state.

Such rights are inherent in the inviolability of the human person. History demonstrates that unless these rights are protected our society's slow, painful progress toward freedom would not have been possible.

The First Amendment Religious Liberty provisions lie close to the heart of the distinctiveness of the American experiment. The uniqueness of the American way of disestablishment and its consequences have often been more obvious to foreign observers such as Alexis de Tocqueville and Lord James Bryce, who wrote that "Of all the differences between the Old world and the New, this is perhaps the most salient." In particular, the Religious Liberty clauses are vital to harnessing otherwise centrifugal forces such as personal liberty and social diversity, thus sustaining republican vitality while making possible a necessary measure of national concord.

The First Amendment Religious Liberty provisions are the democratic world's most salient alternative to the totalitarian repression of human rights and provide a corrective to unbridled nationalism and religious warfare around the world.

The First Amendment Religious Liberty provisions provide the United States' most distinctive answer to one of the world's most pressing questions in the late-twentieth century. They address the problem: How do we live with each other's deepest differences? How do religious convictions and political freedom complement rather than threaten each other on a small planet in a pluralistic age? In a world in which bigotry, fanaticism, terrorism and the state control of religion are all too common responses to these questions, sustaining the justice and liberty of the American arrangement is an urgent moral task.

The First Amendment Religious Liberty provisions give American society a unique position in relation to both the First and Third worlds. Highly modernized like the rest of the First World, yet not so secularized, this society—largely because of religious freedom—remains, like most of the Third World, deeply religious. This fact, which is critical for possibilities of better human understanding, has not been sufficiently appreciated in American self-understanding, or drawn upon in American diplomacy and communication throughout the world.

In sum, as much if not more than any other single provision in the entire Constitution, the Religious Liberty provisions hold the key to American distinctiveness and American destiny. Far from being settled by the interpretations of judges and historians, the last word on the First Amendment likely rests in a chapter yet to be written, documenting the unfolding drama of America. If religious liberty is neglected, all civil liberties will suffer. If it is guarded and sustained, the American experiment will be the more secure.

A TIME FOR REAPPRAISAL

Much of the current controversy about religion and politics neither reflects the highest wisdom of the First Amendment nor serves the best interests of the disputants or the nation. We therefore call for a critical reappraisal of the course and consequences of such controversy. Four widespread errors have exacerbated the controversy needlessly.

The Issue Is Not Only What We Debate, but How

The debate about religion in public life is too often misconstrued as a clash of ideologies alone, pitting "secularists" against the "sectarians" or vice versa. Though competing and even contrary worldviews are involved, the controversy is not solely ideological. It also flows from a breakdown in understanding of how personal and communal beliefs should be related to public life.

The American republic depends upon the answers to two questions. By what ultimate truths ought we to live? And how should these be related to public life? The first question is personal, but has a public dimension because of the connection between beliefs and public virtue. The American answer to the first question is that the government is excluded from giving an answer. The second question, however, is thoroughly public in character, and a public answer is appropriate and necessary to the well-being of this society.

This second question was central to the idea of the First Amendment. The Religious Liberty provisions are not "articles of faith" concerned with the substance of particular doctrines or of policy issues. They are "articles of peace" concerned with the constitutional constraints and the shared prior understanding within which the American

133

people can engage their differences in a civil manner and thus provide for both religious liberty and stable public government.

Conflicts over the relationship between deeply held beliefs and public policy will remain a continuing feature of democratic life. They do not discredit the First Amendment, but confirm its wisdom and point to the need to distinguish the Religious Liberty clauses from the particular controversies they address. The clauses can never be divorced from the controversies they address, but should always be held distinct. In the public discussion, an open commitment to the constraints and standards of the clauses should precede and accompany debate over the controversies.

The Issue Is Not Sectarian, but National

The role of religion in American public life is too often devalued or dismissed in public debate, as though the American people's historically vital religious traditions were at best a purely private matter and at worst essentially sectarian and divisive.

Such a position betrays a failure of civil respect for the convictions of others. It also underestimates the degree to which the Framers relied on the American people's religious convictions to be what Tocqueville described as "the first of their political institutions." In America, this crucial public role has been played by diverse beliefs, not so much despite disestablishment as because of disestablishment.

The Founders knew well that the republic they established represented an audacious gamble against long historical odds. This form of government depends upon ultimate beliefs, for otherwise we have no right to the rights by which it thrives, yet rejects any official formulation of them. The republic will therefore always remain an "undecided experiment" that stands or falls by the dynamism of its non-established faiths.

The Issue Is Larger Than the Disputants

Recent controversies over religion and public life have too often become a form of warfare in which individuals, motives and reputations have been impugned. The intensity of the debate is commensurate with the importance of the issues debated, but to those engaged in this warfare we present two arguments for reappraisal and restraint.

The lesser argument is one of expediency and is based on the ironic fact that each side has become the best argument for the other. One side's excesses have become the other side's arguments; one side's extremists the other side's recruiters. The danger is that, as the ideological warfare becomes self-perpetuating, more serious issues and broader national interests will be forgotten and the bitterness deepened.

The more important argument is one of principle and is based on the fact that the several sides have pursued their objectives in ways which contradict their own best ideals. Too often, for example, religious believers have been uncharitable, liberals have been illiberal, conservatives have been insensitive to tradition, champions of tolerance have been intolerant, defenders of free speech have been censorious, and citizens of a republic based on democratic accommodation have succumbed to a habit of relentless confrontation.

The Issue Is Understandably Threatening

The First Amendment's meaning is too often debated in ways that ignore the genuine grievances or justifiable fears of opposing points of view. This happens when the logic of opposing arguments favors either an unwarranted intrusion of religion into public life or an unwarranted exclusion of religion from it. History plainly shows that with religious control over government, political freedom dies; with political control over religion, religious freedom dies.

The First Amendment has contributed to avoiding both these perils, but this happy experience is no cause for complacency. Though the United States has escaped the worst excesses experienced elsewhere in the world, the republic has shown two distinct tendencies of its own, one in the past and one today.

In earlier times, though lasting well into the twentieth century, there was a *de facto* semi-establishment of one religion in the United States: a generalized Protestantism given dominant status in national institutions, especially in the public schools. This development was largely approved by Protestants, but widely opposed by non-Protestants, including Catholics and Jews.

In more recent times, and partly in reaction, constitutional jurisprudence has tended, in the view of many, to move toward the *de facto* semi-establishment of a wholly secular understanding of the origin, nature and destiny of humankind and of the American nation. During this period, the exclusion of teaching about the role of religion in society, based partly upon a misunderstanding of First Amendment decisions, has ironically resulted in giving a dominant status to such wholly secular understandings in many national institutions. Many secularists appear as unconcerned over the consequences of this development as were Protestants unconcerned about their *de facto* establishment earlier.

Such *de facto* establishments, though seldom extreme, usually benign and often unwitting, are the source of grievances and fears among the several parties in current controversies. Together with the encroachments of the expanding modern state, such *de facto* establishments, as much as any official establishment, are likely to remain a threat to freedom and justice for all.

Justifiable fears are raised by those who advocate theocracy or the coercive power of law to establish a "Christian America." While this advocacy is and should be legally protected, such proposals contradict freedom of conscience and the genius of the Religious Liberty provisions.

At the same time there are others who raise justifiable fears of an unwarranted exclusion of religion from public life. The assertion of moral judgments as though they were morally neutral, and interpretations of the "wall of separation" that would exclude religious expression and argument from public life, also contradict freedom of conscience and the genius of the provisions.

Civility obliges citizens in a pluralistic society to take great care in using words and casting issues. The communications media have a primary role, and thus a special responsibility, in shaping public opinion and debate. Words such as *public, secular* and *religious* should be free from discriminatory bias. "Secular purpose," for example, should not mean "non-religious purpose" but "general public purpose." Otherwise, the impression is gained that "public is equivalent to secular; religion is equivalent to private." Such equations are neither accurate nor just. Similarly, it is false to equate "public" and "governmental." In a society that sets store by the necessary limits on government, there are many spheres of life that are public but non-governmental.

Two important conclusions follow from a reappraisal of the present controversies over religion in public life. First, the process of adjustment and readjustment to the constraints and standards of the Religious Liberty provisions is an ongoing requirement of American democracy. The Constitution is not a self-interpreting, self-executing document; and the prescriptions of the Religious Liberty provisions cannot by themselves resolve the myriad confusions and ambiguities surrounding the right ordering of the relationship between religion and government in a free society. The Framers clearly understood that the Religious Liberty provisions provide the legal construct for what must be an ongoing process of adjustment and mutual give-and-take in a democracy.

We are keenly aware that, especially over state-supported education, we as a people must continue to wrestle with the complex connections between religion and the transmission of moral values in a pluralistic society. Thus, we cannot have, and should not seek, a definitive, once for all solution to the questions that will continue to surround the Religious Liberty provisions.

Second, the need for such a readjustment today can best be addressed by remembering that the two clauses are essentially one provision for preserving religious liberty. Both parts, No establishment and Free exercise, are to be comprehensively understood as being in the service of religious liberty as a positive good. At the heart of the Establishment clause is the prohibition of state sponsorship of religion and at the heart of the Free Exercise clause is the prohibition of state interference with religious liberty.

No sponsorship means that the state must leave to the free citizenry the public expression of ultimate beliefs, religious or otherwise, providing only that no expression is excluded from, and none governmentally favored, in the continuing democratic discourse.

No interference means the assurance of voluntary religious expression free from governmental intervention. This includes placing religious expression on an equal footing with all other forms of expression in genuinely public forums.

No sponsorship and no interference together mean fair opportunity.

That is to say, all faiths are free to enter vigorously into public life and to exercise such influence as their followers and ideas engender. Such democratic exercise of influence is in the best tradition of American voluntarism and is not an unwarranted "imposition" or "establishment."

A TIME FOR RECONSTITUTION

We believe, finally, that the time is ripe for a genuine expansion of democratic liberty, and that this goal may be attained through a new engagement of citizens in a debate that is reordered in accord with constitutional first principles and considerations of the common good. This amounts to no less than the reconstitution of a free republican people in our day. Careful consideration of three precepts would advance this possibility:

The Criteria Must Be Multiple

Reconstitution requires the recognition that the great dangers in interpreting the Constitution today are either to release interpretation from any demanding criteria or to narrow the criteria excessively. The first relaxes the necessary restraining force of the Constitution, while the second overlooks the insights that have arisen from the Constitution in two centuries of national experience.

Religious liberty is the only freedom in the First Amendment to be given two provisions. Together the clauses form a strong bulwark against suppression of religious liberty, yet they emerge from a series of dynamic tensions which cannot ultimately be relaxed. The Religious Liberty provisions grow out of an understanding not only of rights and a due recognition of faiths but of realism and a due recognition of factions. They themselves reflect both faith and skepticism. They raise questions of equality and liberty, majority rule and minority rights, individual convictions and communal tradition.

The Religious Liberty provisions must be understood both in terms of the Framers' intentions and history's sometimes surprising results. Interpreting and applying them today requires not only historical research but moral and political reflection.

The intention of the Framers is therefore a necessary but insufficient criterion for interpreting and applying the Constitution. But applied by itself, without any consideration of immutable principles of justice, the intention can easily be wielded as a weapon for governmental or sectarian causes, some quoting Jefferson and brandishing No establishment and others citing Madison and brandishing Free exercise. Rather, we must take the purpose and text of the Constitution seriously, sustain the principles behind the words and add an appreciation of the many-sided genius of the First Amendment and its complex development over time.

The Consensus Must Be Dynamic

Reconstitution requires a shared understanding of the relationship between the Constitution and the society it is to serve. The Framers understood that the Constitution is more than parchment and ink. The principles embodied in the document must be affirmed in practice by a free people since these principles reflect everything that constitutes the essential forms and substance of their society—the institutions, customs and ideals as well as the laws. Civic vitality and the effectiveness of law can be undermined when they overlook this broader cultural context of the Constitution.

Notable, in this connection is the striking absence today of any national consensus about religious liberty as a positive good. Yet religious liberty is indisputably what the Framers intended and what the First Amendment has preserved. Far from being a matter of exemption, exception or even toleration, religious liberty is an inalienable right. Far from being a sub-category of free speech or a constitutional redundancy, religious liberty is distinct and foundational. Far from being simply an individual right, religious liberty is a positive social good. Far from denigrating religion as a social or political "problem," the separation of Church and State is both the saving of religion from the temptation of political power and an achievement inspired in large part by religion itself. Far from weakening religion, disestablishment has, as an historical fact, enabled it to flourish.

In light of the First Amendment, the government should stand in relation to the churches, synagogues and other communities of faith as

139

the guarantor of freedom. In light of the First Amendment, the churches, synagogues and other communities of faith stand in relation to the government as generators of faith, and therefore contribute to the spiritual and moral foundations of democracy. Thus, the government acts as a safeguard, but not the source, of freedom for faiths, whereas the churches and synagogues act as a source, but not the safeguard, of faiths for freedom.

The Religious Liberty provisions work for each other and for the federal idea as a whole. Neither established nor excluded, neither preferred nor proscribed, each faith (whether transcendent or naturalistic) is brought into a relationship with the government so that each is separated from the state in terms of its institutions, but democratically related to the state in terms of individuals and its ideas.

The result is neither a naked public square where all religion is excluded, nor a sacred public square with any religion established or semi-established. The result, rather, is a civil public square in which citizens of all religious faiths, or none, engage one another in the continuing democratic discourse.

The Compact Must Be Mutual

Reconstitution of a free republican people requires the recognition that religious liberty is a universal right joined to a universal duty to respect that right.

In the turns and twists of history, victims of religious discrimination have often later become perpetrators. In the famous image of Roger Williams, those at the helm of the Ship of State forget they were once under the hatches. They have, he said, "One weight for themselves when they are under the hatches, and another for others when they come to the helm." They show themselves, said James Madison, "as ready to set up an establishment which is to take them in as they were to pull down that which shut them out." Thus, benignly or otherwise, Protestants have treated Catholics as they were once treated, and secularists have done likewise with both.

Such inconsistencies are the natural seedbed for the growth of a *de facto* establishment. Against such inconsistencies we affirm that a right for one is a right for another and a responsibility for all. A right for a

Protestant is a right for an Orthodox is a right for a Catholic is a right for a Jew is a right for a Humanist is a right for a Mormon is a right for a Muslim is a right for a Buddhist—and for the followers of any other faith within the wide bounds of the republic.

That rights are universal and responsibilities mutual is both the premise and the promise of democratic pluralism. The First Amendment, in this sense, is the epitome of public justice and serves as the golden rule for civic life. Rights are best guarded and responsibilities best exercised when each person and group guards for all others those rights they wish guarded for themselves. Whereas the wearer of the English crown is officially the Defender of the Faith, all who uphold the American Constitution are defenders of the rights of all faiths.

From this axiom, that rights are universal and responsibilities mutual, derives guidelines for conducting public debates involving religion in a manner that is democratic and civil. These guidelines are not, and must not be, mandated by law. But they are, we believe, necessary to reconstitute and revitalize the American understanding of the role of religion in a free society.

First, those who claim the right to dissent should assume the responsibility to debate: Commitment to democratic pluralism assumes the coexistence within one political community of groups whose ultimate faith commitments may be incompatible, yet whose common commitment to social unity and diversity does justice to both the requirements of individual conscience and the wider community. A general consent to the obligations of citizenship is therefore inherent in the American experiment, both as a founding principle ("We the people") and as a matter of daily practice.

There must always be room for those who do not wish to participate in the public ordering of our common life, who desire to pursue their own religious witness separately as conscience dictates. But at the same time, for those who do wish to participate, it should be understood that those claiming the right to dissent should assume the responsibility to debate. As this responsibility is exercised, the characteristic American formula of individual liberty complemented by respect for the opinions of others permits differences to be asserted, yet a broad, active community of understanding to be sustained.

Second, those who claim the right to criticize should assume the respon-

sibility to comprehend: One of the ironies of democratic life is that freedom of conscience is jeopardized by false tolerance as well as by outright intolerance. Genuine tolerance considers contrary views fairly
and judges them on merit. Debased tolerance so refrains from making
any judgment that it refuses to listen at all. Genuine tolerance honestly
weighs honest differences and promotes both impartiality and pluralism. Debased tolerance results in indifference to the differences that
vitalize a pluralistic democracy.

Central to the difference between genuine and debased tolerance is
the recognition that peace and truth must be held in tension. Pluralism
must not be confused with, and is in fact endangered by, philosophical
and ethical indifference. Commitment to strong, clear philosophical
and ethical ideas need not imply either intolerance or opposition to
democratic pluralism. On the contrary, democratic pluralism requires
an agreement to be locked in public argument over disagreements of
consequence within the bonds of civility.

The right to argue for any public policy is a fundamental right for
every citizen; respecting that right is a fundamental responsibility for
all other citizens. When any view is expressed, all must uphold as
constitutionally protected its advocate's right to express it. But others
are free to challenge that view as politically pernicious, philosophically
false, ethically evil, theologically idolatrous, or simply absurd, as the
case may be seen to be.

Unless this tension between peace and truth is respected, civility
cannot be sustained. In that event, tolerance degenerates into either
apathetic relativism or a dogmatism as uncritical of itself as it is un-
comprehending of others. The result is a general corruption of principled public debate.

*Third, those who claim the right to influence should accept the responsi-
bility not to inflame:* Too often in recent disputes over religion and public affairs, some have insisted that any evidence of religious influence
on public policy represents an establishment of religion and is therefore precluded as an improper "imposition." Such exclusion of religion
from public life is historically unwarranted, philosophically inconsistent and profoundly undemocratic. The Framers' intention is indisputably ignored when public policy debates can appeal to the theses of
Adam Smith and Karl Marx, or Charles Darwin and Sigmund Freud

but not to the Western religious tradition in general and the Hebrew and Christian Scriptures in particular. Many of the most dynamic social movements in American history, including that of civil rights, were legitimately inspired and shaped by religious motivation.

Freedom of conscience and the right to influence public policy on the basis of religiously informed ideas are inseverably linked. In short, a key to democratic renewal is the fullest possible participation in the most open possible debate.

Religious liberty and democratic civility are also threatened, however, from another quarter. Overreacting to an improper veto on religion in public life, many have used religious language and images not for the legitimate influencing of policies but to inflame politics. Politics is indeed an extension of ethics and therefore engages religious principles; but some err by refusing to recognize that there is a distinction, though not a separation, between religion and politics. As a result, they bring to politics a misplaced absoluteness that idolizes politics, "Satanizes" their enemies and politicizes their own faith.

Even the most morally informed policy positions involve prudential judgments as well as pure principle. Therefore, to make an absolute equation of principles and policies inflates politics and does violence to reason, civil life and faith itself. Politics has recently been inflamed by a number of confusions: the confusion of personal religious affiliation with qualification or disqualification for public office; the confusion of claims to divine guidance with claims to divine endorsement; and the confusion of government neutrality among faiths with government indifference or hostility to religion.

Fourth, those who claim the right to participate should accept the responsibility to persuade: Central to the American experience is the power of political persuasion. Growing partly from principle and partly from the pressures of democratic pluralism, commitment to persuasion is the corollary of the belief that conscience is inviolable, coercion of conscience is evil, and the public interest is best served by consent hard won from vigorous debate. Those who believe themselves privy to the will of history brook no argument and need never tarry for consent. But to those who subscribe to the idea of government by the consent of the governed, compelled beliefs are a violation of first principles. The natural logic of the Religious Liberty provisions is to foster a political culture of persuasion which admits the challenge of opinions from all sources.

Arguments for public policy should be more than private convictions shouted out loud. For persuasion to be principled, private convictions should be translated into publicly accessible claims. Such public claims should be made publicly accessible for two reasons: first, because they must engage those who do not share the same private convictions, and second, because they should be directed toward the common good.

RENEWAL OF FIRST PRINCIPLES

We who live in the third century of the American republic can learn well from the past as we look to the future. Our Founders were both idealists and realists. Their confidence in human abilities was tempered by their skepticism about human nature. Aware of what was new in their times, they also knew the need for renewal in times after theirs. "No free government, or the blessings of liberty," wrote George Mason in 1776, "can be preserved to any people, but by a firm adherence to justice, moderation, temperance, frugality, and virtue, and by frequent recurrence to fundamental principles."

True to the ideals and realism of that vision, we who sign this Charter, people of many and various beliefs, pledge ourselves to the enduring precepts of the First Amendment as the cornerstone of the American experiment in liberty under law.

We address ourselves to our fellow citizens, daring to hope that the strongest desire of the greatest number is for the common good. We are firmly persuaded that the principles asserted here require a fresh consideration, and that the renewal of religious liberty is crucial to sustain a free people that would remain free. We therefore commit ourselves to speak, write and act according to this vision and these principles. We urge our fellow citizens to do the same.

To agree on such guiding principles and to achieve such a compact will not be easy. Whereas a law is a command directed to us, a compact is a promise that must proceed freely from us. To achieve it demands a measure of the vision, sacrifice and perseverance shown by our Founders. Their task was to defy the past, seeing and securing religious liberty against the terrible precedents of history. Ours is to challenge the future, sustaining vigilance and broadening protections against every new menace, including that of our own complacency. Knowing the unquenchable desire for freedom, they lit a beacon. It is for us who know its blessings to keep it burning brightly.

Notes

Introduction by Os Guinness

1. John Courtney Murray, "The Return to Tribalism," an address to the John A. Ryan Forum, April 14, 1961, in *The Catholic Mind*, vol. 60 (January 1962), p. 6.

2. *The Williamsburg Charter Survey on Religion and Public Life* (Washington: Williamsburg Charter Foundation, 1988).

3. Harold L. Hodgkinson, *California: The State and Its Educational System* (Washington: Institute for Educational Leadership, 1986), p. 3.

4. Harold L. Hodgkinson, *All One System: Demographics of Education, Kindergarten through Graduate School* (Washington: Institute for Educational Leadership, 1985).

5. Walter Lippmann, "The Living Past," *Today and Tomorrow*, April 13, 1943; and Clinton Rossiter and James Lave, eds., *The Essential Lippmann* (Harvard University Press, 1982), pp. 206–07.

6. See John Rawls, "The Idea of an Overlapping Consensus," *Oxford Journal of Legal Studies*, vol. 7, no. 1 (1987), pp. 13–195.

7. John Courtney Murray, *We Hold These Truths: Catholic Reflections on the American Proposition* (Sheed and Ward, 1960), p. 195.

8. Alexis de Tocqueville, *Recollections*, ed. J. P. Mayer, trans. George Lawrence (Doubleday, 1970), p. 55.

The Moral Project of the American Founders
by William Lee Miller

1. Douglas Southall Freeman, *George Washington*, vol. 5 (Scribner, 1948–57), pp. 430–36.

2. James Thomas Flexner, *Washington: The Indispensable Man* (New American Library, 1974), pp. 177–78.

3. Flexner, *Washington*, pp. 177–78.

4. H. Richard Niebuhr, *The Meaning of Revelation* (MacMillan, 1941), pp. 59–63.

5. Henry F. May, *The Enlightenment in America* (Oxford University Press, 1976), p. 88.

6. Forrest McDonald, *Novus Ordo Seclorum: The Intellectual Origins of the Constitution* (Kansas University Press, 1985), p. 10.

7. Adrienne Koch, *Power, Morals, and the Founding Fathers* (Cornell University Press, 1961), p. 12.

8. Charles Adams, ed., *The Works of John Adams,* vol. 3 (Little, Brown and Co., 1865), p. 200.

9. John Adams, "Thoughts on Government," in *Political Writings of John Adams,* ed. George A. Peek, Jr. (Macmillan, 1954), p. 83

10. By Douglas Adair in "James Madison," most conveniently found in *Fame and the Founding Fathers* (W. W. Norton, 1974). This quotation is on page 134. I first learned about it from reading Garry Wills.

11. Did they learn deeply from the ancient classics they so often quoted? Bailyn says no. For the most part it was window dressing. Gordon Wood and Forrest McDonald—dealing to be sure with slightly different groups and spans of time from each other and from Bailyn—give a little more weight to the classics in the actual mind of the Americans. See Bernard Bailyn, *The Ideological Origins of the American Revolution* (Harvard University Press, 1967); and Gordon Wood, *The Creation of the American Republic, 1776–1787* (W. W. Norton, 1972).

12. R. R. Palmer, *Twelve Who Ruled* (Princeton University Press, 1969).

13. Adam Michnic, "Letter from the Gdansk Prison," *New York Review of Books,* July 18, 1985.

14. Madison's "Notes of Debates in the Federal Convention," as printed in Wenton U. Sloberg, ed., *The Federal Convention and the Union of the American States* (Bobbs-Merrill, 1958). (Sloberg uses the text edited by Gailland Hunt and James Brown Scott.)

15. McDonald, *Novus Ordo Seclorum,* p. 7.

16. John Courtney Murray, *We Hold These Truths: Catholic Reflections on the American Proposition* (Sheed and Ward, 1960), p. 31.

Religious Freedom and the Challenge of the Modern State by Harold J. Berman

1. Cf. Irving Brant, "Madison: On the Separation of Church and State," *William and Mary Quarterly,* third series, vol. 8, no. 1 (1951), p. 3. Despite Brant's title, none of his numerous citations of Madison includes the phrase "church and state." For example, he quotes Madison's "Essay on Monopolies," written some time after 1817, stating that "the separation between religion and government" is "strongly guarded . . . in the Constitution of the United States."

2. John T. Noonan, Jr., *The Believers and the Powers That Are* (Macmillan, 1987), p. xvi.

3 "At the time of the Revolution, at least 75 percent of American citizens had grown up in families espousing some form of Puritanism." A. James Reichley, *Religion in American Public Life* (Brookings, 1985), p. 53.

4. See John Witte, Jr., "Blest Be the Ties That Bind: Covenant and Community in Puritan Thought," *Emory Law Journal*, vol. 36, no. 2 (1987), pp. 579, 580–81.

5. James Madison, "Memorial and Remonstrance against Religious Assessments, 1785," sec. 1, in Gailland Hunt, ed., *Writings of James Madison*, vol. 2 (G. P. Putnam's Sons, 1901), pp. 183–91.

6. *Caminetti* v. *United States*, 242 U.S. 470, 487 (1917), quoting *Murphy* v. *Ramsey*, 114 U.S. 15, 45, (1885).

7. W. Rogers, "A Treatise on the Law of Domestic Relations, 1899," quoted in John Witte, Jr., "The Reformation of Marriage Law in Martin Luther's Germany: Its Significance Then and Now," *Journal of Law and Religion*, vol. 4, no. 2 (1986), pp. 293, 347.

8. See sources cited in Witte, "Reformation of Marriage Law." In the following pages of his article, Witte goes on to show the transformation of these marriage laws and concepts in the twentieth century.

9. As secretary of the Massachusetts Board of Education, established in 1837 owing in large part to his inspiration, Horace Mann (1796–1859) gave a lecture at a convention held in each county throughout the state for the purpose of explaining the aims, costs, and benefits of education. Lecture V, given in 1841, contains the following excerpt: "As educators, . . . our great duty is . . . to awaken the faculty of thought in all the children of the Commonwealth; . . . to cultivate in them a sacred regard to truth; . . . to train them up to the love of God and the love of Man; to make the perfect example of Jesus Christ lovely in their eyes; and to give to all so much religious instruction as is compatible with the rights of others and with the genius of our government, leaving to parents and guardians the direction, during their school-going days, of all special and peculiar instruction respecting politics and theology; and at last, when the children arrive at years of maturity, to commend them to that inviolable prerogative of private judgment and of self-direction, which, in a Protestant and Republican country, is the acknowledged birth-right of every human being." Horace Mann, *Lectures on Education*, Lecture V, "An Historical View of Education; Showing Its Dignity and Its Degradation."

10. Northwest Ordinance of 1787, art. III, 1 Stat. 50, 51–53 (1789).

11. See A. James Reichley, *Religion in American Public Life* (Brookings, 1985), p. 136.

12. Anson P. Stokes, *Church and State in the United States*, vol. 1 (Harper and Brothers, 1950), pp. 629–30.

13. Stokes, *Church and State*, pp. 636–37.

14. Cf. George C. Mason, editor and transcriber, *The Colonial Vestry Book of Lynnhaven Parish, Princess Anne County, Virginia, 1723–1786* (Newport News, Virginia: George C. Mason, 1949), pp. vii, 113–14.

15. Cf. Louis B. Wright, *The Cultural Life of the American Colonies 1607–1763* (Harper and Brothers, 1957), pp. 23–27.

16. See John Alexander, *Render Them Submissive: Responses to Poverty in Philadelphia, 1760–1800* (University of Massachusetts Press, 1980), pp. 122ff.

17. See Harry S. Stout, *The New England Soul: Preaching and Religious Culture in Colonial New England* (Oxford University Press, 1986). Professor Stout in this book confines himself to the colonial period. However, the practice of preaching "occasional" sermons at public events continued into the nineteenth century.

18. Act of Aug. 7, 1789, ch. 8, 1 Stat. 50 (1789).

19. Act of April 21, 1792, ch. 25, 1 Stat. 257 (1792); Act of Feb. 20, 1833, ch. 42, 4 Stat. 618 (1833). See Noonan, *Believers*, p. 138.

20. Jefferson's letter to the Senate, presenting the treaty with the Kaskaskia Indians for ratification, together with articles 1–7 of the treaty, are reproduced in Robert Cord, *The Separation of Church and State* (Lambeth Press, 1982), pp. 261–63. Article 3 states " *And whereas* the greater part of the said tribe have been baptised and received into the Catholic church, to which they are much attached, the United States will give, annually, for seven years, one hundred dollars towards the support of a priest of that religion, who will engage to perform for said tribe the duties of his office, and also to instruct as many of their children as possible, in the rudiments of literature. And the United States will further give the sum of three hundred dollars, to assist the said tribe in the erection of a church."

21. *Worcester* v. *Georgia*, 31 U.S. (6 Pet) 515 (1832).

22. Examples are given in H. J. Berman, "Religion and Law: The First Amendment in Historical Perspective," *Emory Law Journal*, vol. 35, no. 4 (1986), p. 777–78.

23. See generally J. Bruce Nichols, *The Uneasy Alliance: Religion, Refugee Work and U.S. Foreign Policy* (Oxford University Press, 1988).

24. Milosz said, "The basic issue of the twentieth century is that the state has eaten up all the substance of society." See Nathan Gardels, "An Interview with Czeslaw Milosz," *New York Review of Books*, February 27, 1986, p. 34.

25. Madison wrote to Thomas Ritchie in 1821 that "the legitimate meaning of the Instrument must be derived from the text itself; or if a key is to be sought elsewhere, it must be, not in the opinions or intentions of the body which planned and proposed the Constitution, but in the sense attached to it by the people in their respective State Conventions, where it received all the authority it possesses." *Letters and Other Writings of James Madison*, published by order of Congress, vol. 3 (Philadelphia: J. B. Lippincott and Co., 1867), p. 228. See B. Nelson Ong,

"James Madison on Constitutional Interpretation," *Benchmark*, vol. 3, nos. 1 and 2 (1987), pp. 17ff.

26. In *Wallace* v. *Jaffree*, 472 U.S. 38 (1985), at 52–53. Justice John Paul Stevens analogized the free exercise of religion to the right to speak or to refrain from speaking, stating that "the individual freedom of conscience protected by the First Amendment embraces the right to select any religious faith or none at all." It is highly doubtful, however, that most religious believers would agree that they once "selected" a religious faith or that their continual adherence to a religious faith is basically a matter of individual choice.

27. Charles Adams, ed., *The Works of John Adams*, vol. 9 (Little, Brown and Co., 1865), p. 229.

28. *State* v. *Ambs*, 20 Mo. 214, 216–217 (1854).

29. Madison stated that the right to free exercise of religion is founded on the duty of every man toward God "to render him such homage, and such only, as he believes to be acceptable to him. This duty is precedent, both in order of time and degree of obligation, to the claims of Civil Society. Before any man can be considered as a member of Civil Society, he must be considered as a subject of the Governor of the Universe. . . . We maintain, therefore, that in matters of Religion, no man's right is abridged by the institution of Civil Society, and that Religion is wholly exempt from its cognizance." Madison, *Memorial and Remonstrance against Religious Assessments*, pp. 184–85. Madison's reference to the distinction between man as "a member of Civil Society" and man as "a subject of the Governor of the Universe" is an implicit reference to Lutheran theories of the "two kingdoms," the heavenly and the earthly, and to the Calvinist doctrine of two covenants, one between God and man, and the other between government and people. See Berman, *Religion and Law*, p. 787.

Religious Freedom and the Challenge of Modern Pluralism by James Davison Hunter

1. These figures are taken from Gallup, *Religion in America*. The most recent data came from *The Williamsburg Charter Survey on Religion and American Public Life* (Washington: Williamsburg Charter Foundation, 1988).

2. See the evidence reviewed in J. D. Hunter, *Culture Wars: The Struggle to Define America*, forthcoming, 1990.

3. In the substantive approach the differentia is the category of the "sacred" or the "holy." Yet the sacred, from this perspective, has a fairly specific meaning. The sacred is the realm of the supramundane or the transcendent—what Rudolf Otto called the "mysterium tremendum." As such it is a reality that humans experience as "wholly other" for it evokes feelings of ineffable wonder and awe. Religion, then, is the meaning system that emanates from the sacred. Rudolph

Otto, *The Idea of the Holy*, trans. John W. Harvey (Oxford University Press, 1958).

4. The functional approach, on the other hand, is concerned with religion's role and consequences for individual and social existence. For the individual, religion provides "road maps for the soul"—a meaning system offering a sense of purpose and meaning to the life course, a stable set of moral coordinates to guide everyday life as well as mechanisms to help the individual cope with the traumatic experiences of suffering, pain, and death. At the societal level, religion functions to justify institutional arrangements thereby generating social integration (or in Marxist terminology, to legitimate the status quo). At this level, religion can also perform a prophetic function, delegitimating the status quo and calling for the establishment of a new social order. From this perspective, religion is also defined by the sacred but the sacred in this case could be any ultimate value or any orienting principle adhered to by a social group.

5. Though analytically distinct, these approaches are clearly not mutually exclusive. The substantive approach recognizes the functionality of religion and the functional approach recognizes the special qualities of the supernatural.

6. Even those who are committed in principle to a more substantive approach to religion recognize the profoundly religious nature of these phenomena and employ these terms to describe them.

7. The substantive approach derives from the theoretical tradition of the German phenomenology—the tradition of the *Religionswissenschaften* (most notably developed by such intellectuals as Max Weber, Rudolf Otto, Gerardus Van der Leeuw, Jaochim Wach, and Peter Berger). The functionalist approach derives from French and British structuralism—as found in the works of Emile Durkheim, Branislaw Malinowski, A. R. Radcliffe-Brown, Talcott Parsons, Milton Yinger, Robert Bellah, Thomas Luckmann, and Mary Douglas—and German sociological materialism (Marx, Engels, and most recently, Michael Harrington).

8. This section of the chapter draws in part from chap. 7 of my manuscript, *Culture Wars: The Struggle to Define America*.

9. The reference comes from Laurence Tribe who wrote, "at least through the nineteenth century, religion was given a fairly narrow reading . . . 'religion' referred to theistic notions respecting divinity, morality, and worship." Tribe, *American Constitutional Law* (Foundation Press, 1978), p. 826.

10. *Davis* v. *Beason*, 133 U.S. 333, 341, 342, (1890).

11. *Church of the Holy Trinity* v. *United States*, 143 U.S. 457, 472 (1892).

12. *Davis* v. *Beason*, 133 U.S. at 333, 343.

13. *United States* v. *Macintosh*, 283 U.S. 605, 633–34 (1931).

14. *United States* v. *Kauten*, 133 F. 2d 703, 708 (2d Circ. 1943) (emphasis added).

15. The case was *United States* v. *Ballard*, 322 U.S. 78 (1944).

16. *Torcaso* v. *Watkins*, 367 U.S. 488, 490 (1961).

17. *Torcaso* v. *Watkins*, 367 U.S. at 495.

18. *United States* v. *Seeger*, 380 U.S. 163, 166 (1965).

19. *United States* v. *Seeger*, 380 U.S. at 163, 176.

20. In his book, *A Common Faith* (Yale University Press, 1938), the American philosopher John Dewey insisted that his secular and humanistic beliefs constituted a religious faith. Likewise, the *Humanist Manifesto I* (of 1933) was replete with references and inferences that humanism is a religion. Indeed, in this document it was implied that humanism was the highest realization of man's religious aspirations.

Today man's larger understanding of the universe, his scientific achievements, and his deeper appreciation of brotherhood, have created a situation which requires a new statement of the means and purposes of religion. Such a vital, fearless, and frank religion capable of furnishing adequate social goals and personal satisfactions may appear to many people as a complete break with the past. While this age does owe a vast debt to traditional religions, it is none the less obvious that any religion that can hope to be a synthesizing and dynamic force for today must be shaped for the needs of this age. To establish such a religion is a major necessity of the present. It is a responsibility which rests upon this generation. Religion consists of those actions, purposes, and experiences which are humanly significant. Nothing human is alien to the religious. It includes labor, art, science, philosophy, love, friendship, recreation—all that is in its degree expressive of intelligently satisfying human living. The distinction between the sacred and the secular can no longer be maintained.

Beyond this, Ethical Culture has since 1887 described itself as a "religious fellowship" as has the Fellowship of Religious Humanists (since 1963).

21. This section derivies in part from J. D. Hunter, "America's Fourth Faith: A Sociological Perspective on Secular Humanism," *This World*, vol. 19 (Fall 1987), pp. 101–10.

22. The suggestion that the Unitarian Universalist Association does not really belong to the "family" of organizations of humanism does not hold up in the face of the evidence: J. Gordon Melton's *Encyclopedia of Religion*, a standard reference in almost any academic library, lists the Unitarian Universalist Association in the same cluster of religious organizations as the other humanistic organizations. (Melton labels these the "liberal family" of denominations.) Numerous representatives of the UUA signed the *Humanist Manifesto I* (14), the *Humanist Manifesto II*, and *A Secular Humanist Declaration*. Humanist organizations and conferences welcome the involvement of Unitarian Universalists. (For example the Northeast Regional Humanist Weekend, October, 31 to November 2, 1986, was

sponsored in part by the Community Unitarian Church of White Plains.) Not least, an empirical study by Robert Tapp showed that a majority of Unitarian Universalists felt that the UUA thought of their faith as evolving "closer to a distinctive, humanistic religion" than to liberalism, Protestantism, the ecumenical movement within Christianity, or to an emerging universal religion. See Tapp, *Religion among the Unitarian Universalists* (New York: Seminar Press, 1973), p. 20. As Paul H. Beattie, president of the Fellowship of Religious Humanism put it, "Unitarian Universalists, using the religious model, have led more people to humanism than has the American Humanist Association, Ethical Culture, and the Fellowship of Religious Humanists combined." See Beattie, "The Religion of Secular Humanism," *Free Inquiry*, vol. 6, no. 1 (1985–86), pp. 12–17, cited on p. 16. Finally, humanist spokesman Corliss Lamont acknowledged the role of Unitarians and Universalists in the development of humanism historically. He concluded that "a large portion of the Unitarian churches in the United States are acknowledgedly Humanist." See Lamont, *The Philosophy of Humanism* (Frederick Ungar, 1985), p. 54.

23. These figures were taken from the *Encyclopedia of Associations*. Other humanist organizations that could be mentioned include the Better Humanity League, the Churchman Associates, the Comenius World Council, the National Service Conference of the American Ethical Union, United Focus, the International Humanist and Ethical Union, the Quest National Center, the American Institute for Character Education, the Association for Humanistic Education, and the Association for Humanistic Psychology.

24. There are other creedal formulations of humanism than those found in *The Secular Humanist Declaration*, a *Humanist Manifesto I*, and a *Humanist Manifesto II*. For example, in chap. 9 of his book, *In Defense of Secular Humanism* (Buffalo: Prometheus Books, 1983), Paul Kurtz (a coauthor of a *Humanist Manifesto II* and drafter of *The Secular Humanist Declaration*) summarizes the creedal position this way: "Is it possible to find a common ground between various forms of humanism? It should be clear that there is no essence to which the term humanism corresponds. Rather, any definition of humanism can only be roughly drawn by reference to certain generic philosophical tendencies that humanists have manifested. Humanists, even though of different philosophical persuasions, nevertheless share some basic characteristics. There are, I submit, at least two such minimal principles. First, humanists reject any supernatural conception of the universe; they are sympathetic to one form or another of atheism, agnosticism, or skepticism. Second, humanists affirm that ethical values do not have a supernatural source and have no meaning independent of human experience; humanism is an ethical philosophy in which human beings are central. There are two additional principles to which many, though not all, humanists are attached. Third, there is some commitment to the use of critical reason in the analysis, evaluation, and appraisal of value judgments; and fourth, there is a humanitarian concern for humanity, in both social and individual terms" (p. 64).

Compare also the list of Ethical Ideals listed in the September 1986 newsletter of the Washington Ethical Society for an example of the way in which the Ethical Culture Society would formulate their creed. Also see Frederick Edwords, "The Humanist Philosophy in Perspective," *Humanist*, vol. 44 (January–February 1984), pp. 17–20, 42, for a clarification of the creedal position of the American Humanist Association. Not least, compare these statements to the creedal statement provided by humanist spokesman Corliss Lamont in *The Philosophy of Humanism*, pp. 11–19. The substantive overlap is significant.

25. These figures were taken from *IMF Directory of Publications*, 1986. As of 1980, *Progressive World* ceased to publish.

26. These are mainly in the major metropolitan areas. For example, the 1985 Pacific Bell Telephone Book lists in its yellow pages for Los Angeles, "Churches-Ethical Culture Society" (under which is the listing for the Ethical Culture Society of Los Angeles) and "Churches-Humanist" (under which is the listing for the Humanist Church of Religious Science). In the Chesapeake and Potomac Telephone Company yellow pages for Washington, D.C., there is also a listing, "Churches-Ethical Culture Society" (under which is the listing for the Washington Ethical Society and Humanists of Washington, Inc.). And in the NYNEX telephone book for Manhattan, there is a listing for a "Church of Humanism and Humanist Theological Center." In all of these cases, the yellow page listing is free for the organization and the location of the listing (under the category of Churches) is approved by the humanist organizations. If they disapprove of the location, they can have it removed.

27. This according to the *Encyclopedia of Associations* and the preamble of the American Humanist Association (AHA).

28. The interrelatedness of these organizations as a social network could be documented extensively. I will only mention a few pieces of evidence. For one, representatives of many of these groups signed the Manifestos and the Declaration. Second, according to the *Encyclopedia of Associations*, the AHA is formally affiliated with the Fellowship of Religious Humanists and the International Humanist and Ethical Union; and the Council for Democratic and Secular Humanism, the Fellowship of Religious Humanists, the American Ethical Union, and the Washington Ethical Society are with the International Humanist and Ethical Union and, as such, with each other. Third, at a conference held in the fall of 1986 (mentioned in note 3), the sponsors included the American Ethical Union, the American Humanist Association, the Community Unitarian Church of White Plains, the Council for Democratic and Secular Humanism, the Fellowship of Religious Humanists, the International Humanist and Ethical Union, the North American Committee for Humanism, the Northeast District of the AHA, and the Westchester Ethical Humanist Society. See *Free Mind*, vol. 29 (September/October, 1986), p. 1. Fourth, Tapp, *Religion among the Unitarian Universalists*, notes that "the Ethical Societies (represented by the American Ethical Union), the American Humanist Association, and the Unitarian Universalist Association

pooled personnel for a common Washington legislative office in 1970"(p.63). Finally, humanist spokesman Corliss Lamont summarily describes the humanist network in his book, *The Philosophy of Humanism*, pp. 19–29.

29. All quotations here are taken from the *Humanist Manifesto II*.

30. Donald Stone, "The Human Potential Movement," in Charles Glock and Robert Bellah, eds., *The New Religious Consciousness* (University of California Press, 1976), p. 98.

31. Compare the analysis of the three major humanist documents, almost any issue of the *Humanist*, and the mass direct mailings with the criteria of sectarianism set out by Peter Berger, "The Sociological Study of Sectarianism," *Social Research*, vol. 21 (Winter 1954).

32. See Dewey, *A Common Faith*; Lamont, *The Philosophy of Humanism*; Kurtz, *In Defense of Secular Humanism*; and Beattie, "The Religion of Secular Humanism."

33. Talcott Parsons, *Action Theory* (Free Press, 1978), pp. 308ff., 249ff.

34. On elites in general, see Research and Forecasts, *The Connecticut Mutual Life Report on Values in the 80s* (Research and Forecasts, 1980). On media elites, see the comprehensive review in Stanley Rothman, "The Mass Media in Post-Industrial America," in S. M. Lipset, ed., *The Third Century* (University of Chicago Press, 1979). On the professoriate, see Seymour Martin Lipset, "The New Class and the Professoriate," in B. Bruce-Briggs, ed., *The New Class?* (Transaction Books, 1979).

35. Peter Berger, "Religion and the American Future," in S. M. Lipset, ed., *The Third Century*, and "The Worldview of the New Class: Secularity and Its Discontents," in B. Bruce-Briggs, ed., *The New Class?*

36. Alvin Gouldner, *The Future of Intellectuals and the Rise of the New Class* (Oxford: Oxford University Press, 1978).

37. The inclusion of all theists is not arbitrary for the suit was defined as a class action suit on behalf of "all theists."

38. Other support came from the pro bono assistance of Hogan and Hartson, a large firm in Washington, D.C.

39. One of these studies was conducted by Paul Vitz for the National Institute of Education. Vitz, "Religion and Traditional Values in Public School Textbooks: An Empirical Study," a report submitted to the National Institution of Education (Washington, 1985), and "Religion and Traditional Values in Public School Textbooks," *Public Interest* (Summer 1986), pp. 79–90. Two other studies, one sponsored by People for the American Way and the other by Americans United for the Separation of Church and State, documented the same reality. People for the American Way, *Looking at History* (Washington, 1986); and Charles Haynes, *Teaching about Religious Freedom in America's Secondary Schools* (Washington: Americans United for the Separation of Church and State, 1985).

40. See the following studies conducted by Richard Baer. "Values Clarification

as Indoctrination," *Educational Forum*, vol. 41 (January 1977), pp. 155–65; "Teaching Values in the Schools: Clarification or Indoctrination," *Principal*, vol. 61 (January 1982), pp. 17–21, 36; and "Cosmos, Cosmology, and the Public Schools," *This World* (Spring–Summer 1983), pp. 5–17.

41. Charles Francis Potter, *Humanism, A New Religion* (Simon Schuster, 1930).

42. Paul Blanshard, "Three Cheers for Our Secular State," *The Humanist* (March–April 1976), pp. 17–25.

43. John H. Dunphy, "Public Education," *Humanist* (January–February 1983).

44. Coles's deposition for the state was so damaging to their arguments that he was never called to testify. The plaintiffs, in fact, used Coles's deposition on their own behalf. Coles is here quoted from an article in the *Christian Science Monitor*, March 23, 1987.

45. *Washington Post*, April 5, 1987.

46. Laurence Tribe, *American Constitutional Law* (Mineola, N.Y.: Foundations, 1978), p. 828. The other justification offered is that the First Amendment only mentions the word religion once, with regard to the establishment clause. That it was not mentioned with regard to the free exercise clause allows for a broader interpretation.

Freedom of Conscience or Freedom of Choice?
by Michael J. Sandel

1. This view is elaborated most notably in John Rawls, *A Theory of Justice* (Harvard University Press, 1971), and in his subsequent writings. See also Ronald Dworkin, "Liberalism," in Stuart Hampshire, ed., *Public and Private Morality* (Cambridge University Press, 1978); and Bruce Ackerman, *Social Justice in the Liberal State* (Yale University Press, 1980).

2. Dworkin, "Liberalism," p. 127.

3. George Kateb, "Democratic Individuality and the Claims of Politics," *Political Theory*, vol. 12 (August 1984), p. 343.

4. John Rawls, "Kantian Constructivism in Moral Theory," *Journal of Philosophy*, vol. 77 (September 1980), p. 543.

5. The objection I present here partly summarizes, partly clarifies and extends, an objection developed in Michael Sandel, *Liberalism and the Limits of Justice* (Cambridge University Press, 1983).

6. Rawls, *Theory of Justice*, sec. 18–19.

7. *Abington Township School District* v. *Schempp*, 374 U.S. 203, 226 (1963).

8. *Epperson* v. *Arkansas*, 393 U.S. 97 (1968).

9. *Everson* v. *Board of Education of Ewing Township*, 330 U.S. 1, 24 (1947), Justice Jackson dissenting.

10. *Abington* v. *Schempp*, 374 U.S. at 203, 222.

11. *Walz* v. *Tax Commission of the City of New York*, 397 U.S. 664, 669 (1970).

12. *Wallace* v. *Jaffree*, 105 S.Ct. 2479, 2491, 2492 (1985).

13. See for example John Locke, "A Letter Concerning Toleration," in Charles Sherman, ed., *Treatise of Civil Government and A Letter Concerning Toleration*, 1689 (New York: Appleton Century Crofts, 1965); and John Rawls, "Justice as Fairness: Political not Metaphysical," *Philosophy and Public Affairs*, vol. 14 (Summer 1985), p. 249.

14. *Everson* v. *Board of Education of Ewing Township*, 330 U.S. 1 (1947). The quotation is from Jefferson's letter to the Baptists of Danbury, Connecticut, January 1, 1802. *Writings* (New York: Library of America, 1984), p. 510. (Hereafter *Writings*.)

15. Justice Reed dissenting in *McCollum* v. *Board of Education*, 333 U.S. 203, 247 (1948).

16. *Abington* v. *Schempp*, 374 U.S. at 203, 225.

17. *McCollum* v. *Board of Education*, 333 U.S. at 203, 212.

18. In *Everson* v. *Board of Education*.

19. Article VI.

20. Unlike European religious establishments, the American versions, at least after the Revolution, were multiple rather than exclusive establishments, allowing support for more than a single denomination. Some states established Protestantism, others Christianity, as the religion eligible for tax support. See Leonard W. Levy, *The Establishment Clause* (Macmillan, 1986), chap. 2.

21. See Mark DeWolfe Howe, *The Garden and the Wilderness* (University of Chicago Press, 1965), chap. 1; and Wilbur G. Katz, *Religion and American Constitutions* (Northwestern University Press, 1964), p. 9.

22. *Writings*, p. 347.

23. See Leo Pfeffer, *Church, State and Freedom*, rev. ed. (Beacon Press, 1967), pp. 108–11; and Levy, *Establishment Clause*, pp. 51–61.

24. See Richard E. Morgan, *The Supreme Court and Religion* (Free Press, 1972), pp. 30–31. The Maryland case was Torcaso v. *Watkins*, 367 U.S. 488 (1961).

25. Kent quoted in Leo Pfeffer, *Church, State and Freedom* (Beacon Press, 1967), p. 665.

26. *Permoli* v. *First Municipality of the City of New Orleans*, 3 Howard 589, 671 (1845).

27. Levy, *Establishment Clause*, p. 122.

28. Anson Phelps Stokes and Leo Pfeffer, *Church and State in the United States*, rev. ed. (Harper and Row, 1964), pp. 433–34; Pfeffer, *Church, State and Freedom*, pp. 146–47; and Morgan, *The Supreme Court and Religion*, pp. 50–51.

29. *Reynolds* v. *Reynolds*, 98 U.S. 145, 164 (1878).

30. *Cantwell* v. *Connecticut*, 310 U.S. 296, 302 (1940).

31. *Everson* v. *Board of Education*, 330 U.S. 1.

32. *Everson* v. *Board of Education*, 330 U.S. 1.

33. A recent exception is Justice Rehnquist's dissent in *Wallace* v. *Jaffree*, 105 S.Ct. 2479, 2508 (1985).

34. *Everson* v. *Board of Education*, 330 U.S. 1.

35. *Abington* v. *Schempp*, 374 U.S. at 203, 225.

36. *Abington* v. *Schempp*, 374 U.S. at 203, 313. In *Engel* v. *Vitale*, 370 U.S. 421, 447, 450 (1962), by contrast, Stewart had defended school prayer by appealing not to neutrality but to "the history of the religious traditions of our people" and "the deeply entrenched and highly cherished spiritual traditions of our Nation."

37. *Epperson* v. *Arkansas*, 393 U.S. 97, 113 (1968).

38. *Epperson* v. *Arkansas*, 393 U.S. at 97, 113. The problem Black raises in connection with creationism is analogous to the difficulties posed in chapter 2 about the neutral stance toward witchcraft, abortion, and slavery. See pp. 39–44 above.

39. *Wallace* v. *Jaffree*, 105 S.Ct. 2479, 2491, 2505 (1985). In a separate dissent, Justice Rehnquist challenged the assumption, accepted since *Everson*, that the establishment clause required government to be neutral between religion and irreligion. *Wallace* v. *Jaffree*, 105 S.Ct., at 2512.

40. *McGowan* v. *Maryland*, 366 U.S. 420, 448 (1961).

41. *Lynch* v. *Donnelly*, 465 U.S. 668, 669 (1984). In *Marsh* v. *Chambers*, 463 U.S. 783 (1983), the Court upheld the Nebraska legislature's practice of opening each day with a prayer by a chaplain paid by the state, citing the long history of the practice. Writing in dissent, Justice Brennan construed the decision as carving out a narrow exception to establishment clause doctrine.

42. *McGowan* v. *Maryland*, 366 U.S. at 366, 572, 573.

43. *Lynch* v. *Donnelly*, 465 U.S. at 668, 726–27.

44. *McCollum* v. *Board of Education*, 333 U.S. 203, 212 (1948).

45. *Everson* (Justice Rutledge dissenting).

46. *Abington* v. *Schempp*, 374 U.S. at 203, 246 (Justice Brennan concurring).

47. Roger Williams quoted in H. Howe, *The Garden and the Wilderness*, pp. 5–6.

48. *Engel* v. *Vitale*, 370 U.S. 421, 431–32 (1962).

49. Concurring opinion in *Abington* v. *Schempp*, 374 U.S. at 203, 259.

50. Justice Rutledge dissenting in *Everson*.

51. *McCollum* v. *Board of Education*, 333 U.S. 203, 216, 217 (1948).

52. Justice Black dissenting in *Zorach* v. *Clauson*, 343 U.S. 306, 319 (1952).

53. *Cantwell* v. *Connecticut*, 310 U.S. 296, 303 (1940) (emphasis added).

54. *Abington* v. *Schempp*, 374 U.S. 203, 222, 317 (1963). Justice Clark for the Court, Justice Stewart in dissent.

55. Gail Merel, "The Protection of Individual Choice: A Consistent Under-

standing of Religion under the First Amendment," *University of Chicago Law Review*, vol. 45 (Spring 1978), pp. 805–43, cited on p. 806.

56. Alan Schwarz, "No Imposition of Religion: The Establishment Clause Value," *Yale Law Journal*, vol. 77 (March 1968), pp. 692–737, cited on p. 728.

57. David A. J. Richards, *Toleration and the Constitution* (Oxford University Press, 1986), p. 140.

58. Laurence Tribe, *American Constitutional Law* (Mineola, N.Y.: Foundation Press, 1978), p. 812.

59. *Wallace* v. *Jaffree*, 105 S.Ct. 2479, 2487, 2488 (1985) (emphasis added).

60. *Wolman* v. *Walter*, 433 U.S. 229, 265 (1977), Justice Powell concurring and dissenting. See also Chief Justice Burger's dissent in *Meek* v. *Pittenger*, 421 U.S. 349 (1975).

61. See President Ronald Reagan's "State of the Union Address," January 27, 1987, and generally, Richard E. Morgan, *The Politics of Religious Conflict* (Washington, D.C.: University Press of America, 1980).

62. Tribe, *American Constitutional Law*, p. 885.

63. Justice Stevens's phrase in *Wallace* v. *Jaffree*, 105 S.Ct. 2479, 2488 (1985).

64. Madison, "Memorial and Remonstrance against Religious Assessments," 1785, in Marvin Meyers, ed., *The Mind of the Founder*, rev. ed. (Hanover, N.H.: New England University Press, 1981), pp. 6–13.

65. 1779, in *Writings*, p. 346, Jefferson writes that God "chose not to propagate" religion by coercion, "as was in his Almighty power to do, but extend it by its influence on reason alone."

66. *Writings*, p. 346.

67. In Locke, *Treatise on Civil Government and A Letter Concerning Toleration*, ed. Charles Sherman (New York: Appleton Century Crofts, 1965), p. 204. Jefferson's argument may also have reflected the influence of the eighteenth-century philosopher Francis Hutcheson, whose account of belief is discussed in Morton White, *The Philosophy of the American Revolution* (Oxford University Press, 1978), pp. 195–202.

68. Madison, "Memorial and Remonstrance," p. 7.

69. The phrase is from John Rawls, "Kantian Constructivism in Moral Theory," *Journal of Philosophy*, vol. 77 (September 1980), p. 543.

70. *Thornton* v. *Calder*, 105 S.Ct. 2914 (1985).

71. *Thornton* v. *Calder*, 105 S.Ct. 2914, Burger at 2918, O'Connor at 2919.

72. *Sherbert* v. *Verner*, 374 U.S. 398, 409 (1963). Three justices argued that the decision was inconsistent with *Braunfeld* v. *Brown*, 366 U.S. 599 (1961), where the Court had refused to exempt Orthodox Jewish store owners from Sunday Blue laws, even though this meant they had to forgo business two days each week rather than one.

73. *United States* v. *Seeger,* 380 U.S. 163 (1965).

74. *Gillette* v. *United States,* 401 U.S. 437, 454 (1971). See also *Welsh* v. *United States,* 398 U.S. 333 (1970).

75. *Gillette* v. *United States,* 401 U.S. 437, 454 (1971).

76. *Wisconsin* v. *Yoder* 406 U.S. 205, 216, 220 (1972).

77. *Wisconsin* v. *Yoder* 406 U.S. at 245.

78. *Goldman* v. *Weinberger,* 106 S.Ct. 1310, 1313 (1986).

79. *Goldman* v. *Weinberger,* 106 S.Ct. at 1313–15.

Religion in a Free Society
by Charles Taylor

1. Joseph Schumpeter, *Capitalism, Socialism, and Democracy* (Harper and Row, 1950).

2. Letter to E. Livingston, July 10, 1822, cited in Leonard W. Levy, *The Establishment Clause* (Macmillan, 1986), p. 178.

3. See, for instance, Ronald Dworkin, "Liberalism," in Stuart Hampshire, ed., *Public and Private Morality* (Cambridge University Press, 1978).

4. See Charles Taylor, "Alternative Futures," in Alan Cairns and Cynthia Williams, eds., *Constitutionalism, Citizenship, and Society in Canada* (University of Toronto Press, 1985), for a fuller discussion of this development and the contrast between Canada and the United States in this regard. See also Michael Sandel, "The Procedural Republic and the Unencumbered Self," *Political Theory,* vol. 12 (April 1984), pp. 81–96.

5. See the discussion of this form of individualism and its political consequences in Robert Bellah, *Habits of the Heart* (University of California Press, 1985).

6. Levy, *Establishment Clause,* pp. 162–63.

Contributors

PETER L. BERGER is university professor and director of the Institute for the Study of Economic Culture at Boston University and is the author of *The Sacred Canopy; The Homeless Mind; Pyramids of Sacrifice;* and *The Capitalist Revolution* among others.

HAROLD J. BERMAN is Woodruff Professor of Law at Emory University and is the author of *Law and Revolution.*

OS GUINNESS is the executive director of the Williamsburg Charter Foundation. He is the author of *The Dust of Death; In Two Minds;* and *The Gravedigger File;* and he is a contributor to *America in Perspective.*

JAMES DAVISON HUNTER is professor of sociology and religious studies at the University of Virginia in Charlottesville, Virginia. He is the author of *American Evangelicalism; Evangelicalism: The Coming Generation;* and *Culture Wars: The Struggle to Define America.*

WILLIAM LEE MILLER is White Burkett Miller Professor of Public Affairs at the University of Virginia and is the author of *The First Liberty* among many other books.

MICHAEL J. SANDEL is professor of political philosophy in the Department of Government at Harvard University. He is the author of *Liberalism and the Limits of Justice* and the editor of *Liberalism and Its Critics.*

CHARLES TAYLOR is professor of philosophy and political science at McGill University and is the author of *Explanation of Behavior; Pattern of Politics;* and *Hegel and Modern Society.*

Index